The Little Black Book

The Little Black Book

A Do-It-Yourself Guide
for Law Student Competitions

Barbara K. Bucholtz
Martin A. Frey
Melissa L. Tatum

PROFESSORS OF LAW, UNIVERSITY OF TULSA
COLLEGE OF LAW

CAROLINA ACADEMIC PRESS
Durham, North Carolina

ISBN 0-89089-512-0
LCCN 2001097412

CAROLINA ACADEMIC PRESS
700 Kent Street
Durham, North Carolina 27701
Telephone (919) 489-7486
Fax (919)493-5668
www.cap-press.com

Printed in the United States of America

Contents

Preface

Are you a student participating in a law school competition? A coach of a law school competition team? A law school professor who teaches advocacy skills? Then this book is for you. We have designed *The Little Black Book* to fill a critical niche in law school pedagogy: the skills for succeeding in law school competitions. Law schools perpetually struggle with the need to fit an ever-expanding universe of both doctrinal studies and skills development into a finite curriculum. Training in competition skills inevitably gets squeezed and edited down, and sometimes even left on the cutting room floor. Yet students can benefit enormously from these competitions, as they provide a way for students to practice and develop skills that will benefit themselves and their clients once students enter the workforce.

Some law schools do offer courses in appellate advocacy or require appellate brief writing as part of their various legal writing programs, but these programs are not universal. In addition, the standard law school curriculum has expanded to encompass alternative dispute resolution mechanisms, such as negotiation and mediation, but schools often are not able to offer hands-on instruction in these topics to all students. The end result is that some students may learn the theory, but not necessarily the practical skills that accompany these mechanisms and others may not even learn the theory. Even those schools who do have courses in appellate advocacy, mediation, negotiation, and client counseling often cannot also incorporate the specific skills necessary for succeeding in competitions. (By "success" we mean mastering the skills used in the competition; skills that will serve students well in their chosen profession.) These deficiencies led us to write this book, which is a step-by-step instruction handbook that takes students through the procedures of each style of competition. Each section of this book takes a direct and pragmatic approach that is easily adapted to a broad spectrum of instruction: individual self-teaching, coach-student training, and classroom teaching. At The University of Tulsa College of Law, this book is being used by individual students in preparing briefs for the Stetson, Jessup, and National Native American Law Students Association Moot Court Competitions; by coaches in their respective training programs; and by professors as an instruction manual for appellate advocacy courses.

Part I of this manual is designed to guide the user in applying the analytical, writing and research skills students learned (or are learning) in first year courses to the task of preparing an appellate brief. The manual does presuppose some background in legal analysis and persuasive argument. Part I also instructs students on developing and presenting an oral argument based on their brief. Part II focuses on non-brief writing competitions, specifically the Client Counseling, Negotiation, and Mediation Competitions.

About the Authors

The authors of *The Little Black Book: A Do-It-Yourself Guide for Law Student Competitions* are Barbara K. Bucholtz, Martin A. Frey and Melissa L. Tatum.

Barbara K. Bucholtz is an Associate Professor of Law at The University of Tulsa College of Law where she has served for several years as the faculty advisor for The University of Tulsa's Jessup Teams. She regularly teaches courses in Contracts, Corporations, Nonprofit Law and Legal Analysis and Writing. She is Director of the University's Nonprofit Law Center. For four years, she served as senior law clerk for the Honorable James O. Ellison, Chief Judge of the United States District Court, Northern District of Oklahoma. Prior to her clerkship, she was a practicing attorney in Chicago and Tulsa law firms. Her legal scholarship focuses on issues facing for-profit and nonprofit associations.

Martin A. Frey is a Professor Emeritus at The University of Tulsa College of Law. Prior to his retirement, Professor Frey was a Senior Adjunct Settlement Judge for the United States District and Bankruptcy Courts for the Northern District of Oklahoma as well as the Reporter for the Civil Justice Reform Act Advisory Group for the United States District Court for the Northern District of Oklahoma. He was the Co-Director of the Center on Dispute Resolution at the College of Law, the Faculty Advisory to the Board of Advocates (the student umbrella organization that coordinates all competition activities), and the Faculty Coach to several ABA/LSD Negotiation Competition teams. He taught Introduction to ADR; Interviewing, Counseling and Negotiating; Contracts; and Secured Transactions. Professor Frey also drafted the problems for the finals of the 2000–2001 ABA/LSD Negotiation Competition and served as the Faculty Coordinator for the regional 2000–2001 ABA Mediation Competition held at The University of Tulsa. He writes in the areas of ADR, contracts, and bankruptcy law.

Melissa L. Tatum is an Associate Professor at The University of Tulsa College of Law, where she also serves as Co-Director of the Native American Law Center and as Director of the Native American Law Moot Court Programs. As part of her work with the moot court programs, Professor Tatum oversees all aspects of the annual intramural Native American Law Moot Court Competition and serves as primary coach for the teams TU sends to the National NALSA Moot Court Competition. Prior to taking charge of the Native American Law Moot Court Programs, she served as primary coach of the health law moot court teams. Professor Tatum has also judged both local and national moot court competitions. In so doing, she draws heavily on her experience clerking for a U.S. Magistrate Judge and for two federal appellate court judges. Professor Tatum teaches Criminal Procedure: Police Practices, Criminal Procedure: Adjudication, Protection of Minority and Indigenous Cultures, and an American Indian Law Seminar. In addition to her teaching, Professor Tatum has published numerous articles in the fields of Indian law and Section 1983, and regularly lectures at regional and national conferences on Indian law. She also serves as a judge for the Southwest Intertribal Court of Appeals.

Acknowledgments

With appreciation, the authors acknowledge the following individuals for their invaluable contributions to this text:

We are grateful to Professor Judith Royster who initially identified the need for this kind of manual, in connection with her experience in coaching TU's Native American Law Competition team and who has contributed her suggestions on developing an oral argument.

Special thanks to Cyndee Jones, Administrative Faculty Assistant at the law school, who typed much of the manuscript and provided administrative support. Thanks to colleague Doug Todd, coach of TU's Jessup team for his insightful comments.

Professor Bucholtz wishes to thank Erin Baxter, who served as her research assistant during the preparation of the first draft, and all of the students like Gwen Clegg, who used the first draft to prepare for Moot Court competitions and offered their views on its strengths and weaknesses. Special thanks also go to students, like Jesse Sumner, who used the first draft in Professor Bucholtz's legal analysis class and critiqued its efficacy.

Professor Frey would like to thank the members of his Regional Negotiation Teams, Kara L. Horton and Hillary Cinocca, Pam Nix and Richard E. Nantz, and Stephanie M. Johnson and C. Alison Smith, and the members of his Introduction to ADR and Interviewing, Counseling and Negotiating classes.

Professor Tatum would like to thank Heather WhiteMan Runs Him and Natalie Lambreth, of Harvard University Law School, for their permission to reprint a portion of their award-winning brief.

The authors gratefully acknowledge other authors, publishers, and copyright holders who kindly granted permission to reprint excerpts or use concepts from their materials. We expressly wish to acknowledge and thank the following for use of the copyrighted materials:

American Bar Association Section on Dispute Resolution, *Representation in Mediation Advocacy Competition* (2000–2001).

American Bar Association, American Bar Association Law Student Division, *Negotiation Competition Rules and Standards for Judging* (2000–2001).

American Bar Association, American Bar Association Law Student Division, *Client Counseling Competition Rules and Standards for Judging* (2000–2001).

Tulsa Law Review. Martin A. Frey, *Does ADR Offer Second Class Justice?*, 36 Tulsa Law Journal 727 (Summer 2001), and Martin A. Frey, *Representing Clients Effectively in an ADR Environment*, 33 Tulsa Law Journal 443 (Fall 1997).

Part I

Appellate Advocacy Competitions

This part is designed for students participating in the traditional appellate advocacy competitions, in which the competitors write an appellate brief and conduct an oral argument. We've designed this Part to track the process each competitor must follow to develop a brief and argument from the Record.

Chapter 1

Writing the Brief

This chapter is designed to assist students in starting the appellate advocacy competition process. Since the first step must be the brief, that is where we begin.

A. The Role of the Brief

When students get involved in moot court, they often focus on the oral argument. In fact, for many students "moot court" becomes synonymous with "oral argument." The challenge of thinking on your feet, fencing with the judges, and the adrenaline rush are often viewed as the heart and soul of the moot court experience. Students view the brief as a necessary but pesky hurdle to get over quickly so that they can get to the "good part," the oral argument. The brief, however, is a critical component of the moot court experience. Without a good brief, oral argument is worthless, as well as meaningless.

Why is the brief so important? Well, looking at it from a purely pragmatic point of view, in many moot court competitions, the brief score and the oral argument score both count in determining which teams will advance. For example, in several competitions, the oral argument score counts for only sixty percent of the total score for each round. The score on the brief supplies the other forty percent. That forty percent often turns out to be a make-or-break factor. A few years ago, one of The University of Tulsa teams in a competition advanced past the preliminary rounds into the "out rounds" or the elimination rounds. After the first round of "playoffs," the judges explicitly told our team that they out-argued their opponents. Despite the fact that our team was better in the oral argument, however, the opposing team would be the one to advance to the next round of competition. Why? Because the other team's brief score was so much better than our team's brief score that it more than made up for the difference in oral argument points. So don't take the brief lightly — it can literally end your competition prematurely.

A second pragmatic reason for spending time and effort on the brief is that the arguments in the brief should fuel your oral arguments. Written and spoken language are very different, but your oral argument will essentially be a distillation of the key components of your brief. In real life, the case is usually won or lost on the brief. Very rarely does oral argument play a major factor in the outcome of the case. In moot court, oral argument becomes more important, but the points you make in your oral argument are going to come out of your brief. If you have a poorly researched and poorly analyzed brief, you are sunk before you even begin your oral argument. The answers to many of the judges' questions are going to come from your brief — that is where you develop a "knowledge base" of the relevant facts, decisions, doctrines, legal rules, and arguments that you will draw upon in responding both to the judges and to your opponents. If you cheat the brief, you cheat your oral argument.

Finally, from a more selfish perspective, most competitions give awards for best brief. Do a good job on your brief and you maximize the prizes for which you are eligible — you could win the competition, the oralist awards, AND the brief awards. Basically, then, the message is that you *must* put in a great deal of time and effort on the brief, or your moot court experience will not be a very fulfilling one. This manual is a good start to writing a winning brief, but you must also rely on other sources. Go back to your legal research and writing notes. If you didn't cover brief writing in that class, go back and look at your book. Many legal research and writing books have chapters on how to write a brief. Read other briefs from various competitions — read the winning ones, the average ones, and the poorly written ones. Learn what makes a good brief. Write a good brief, and you're on your way to having a great competition. And, now, let's get started.

B. Analysis of the Record, the Issue(s) and the "Local Rules"

In the traditional Moot Court competition, the Record of the case is distributed to the competitors. Begin by studying the entire Record with great care. The Record may include not only documentation concerning the pre-litigation facts from which the legal dispute developed, but documentation regarding the procedural history as well. The Record, in any litigation, is comprised of all instruments filed in the court clerk's office under the case docket number. It may include, in addition to the petition (or complaint) and answer, procedural motions, documentary evidence gleaned from discovery, interlocutory orders, final orders and relevant parts of trial transcripts. On appeal, only the parts of the Record that are relevant to the issue(s) the appellate court will consider are sent up ("certified") to the higher court. In addition to a hypothetical "certified" record, most Moot Court competitions also include a narrative of the facts in the case (both pre-litigation and procedural), the nature of the action, the parties and the posture of the case.

Finally, Moot Court competitions generally include specific instructions ("local rules") about brief preparation and oral argument. With respect to the required format for the brief, some competitions will refer you to another set of court rules (often, those of the U.S. Supreme Court). Make sure you study the local rules and any referenced rules. If your brief does not follow them meticulously, your score will be lowered.

After you have studied the record and the local rules, you should:

- Outline the pre-litigation and procedural facts (including the nature and current posture of the case);
- Identify the appropriate standard and scope of review for the reviewing court and the jurisdictional prerequisites for obtaining review (if it is an appellate case);
- Identify the issue or issues before the court and develop a preliminary theory of the case for each party.

Now, you are ready to begin the Research Process.

C. The Research Process

1. Primary Authority

As you begin the research process, recall that your goal is to find the legal rules that govern the facts of the case: these are called "Primary Authority." Primary Authority differs by jurisdiction. The two jurisdictions of Primary Authority are Domestic Law Primary Authority and International Law Primary Authority. Domestic Law Primary Authority includes constitutions, statutes, regulations, local ordinances and case law interpreting them, as well as common law precepts adopted and construed in court opinions. International Law Primary Authority includes International Law, General Principles of International Law and the writings of highly publicized legal scholars. Article #38 of the International Court of Justice statute contains a commonly accepted list of sources in order of importance.

Recall that primary authority is ordered hierarchically: federal law "trumps" state law when the two conflict, and constitutions take precedence over statutes, while statutes pre-empt conflicting common law precepts, agency regulations and ordinances. Within the International Law arena, generally International Treaties, Protocols and Agreements (to which the two disputing countries are parties) govern the dispute between the countries and act like the "trump," as in domestic federal law. In addition, Customary International Law binds both countries and must not be ignored. Customary International Law may "trump" a legal issue when it is an established practice among the countries of the world, regardless of whether or not the disputing countries have signed an International Treaty binding them to uphold that particular legal rule. Most domestic legal problems involve legal rules drawn from statutes and cases. Most International legal problems involve International Treaties, Protocols and Agreements. The Statute of the International Court of Justice (ICJ) governs cases brought before the ICJ. The ICJ statute can be found on the ICJ website at *http://www.un.org/Overview/Organs/icj.html.*

Publication of Statutes:

Federal statutes are first published individually in pamphlets called "slip laws." They are cumulated chronologically in pamphlets called "advance sheets." They are then bound in chronological order in publications called "statutes-at-large." Finally they are reordered according to subject matter (codified) and officially published in the United States Code (U.S.C.). Unofficial versions are published in the United States Code Annotated (U.S.C.A.) and United States Code Service (U.S.C.S.). Publication of state statutes follows a similar pattern.

Publication of Cases:

Both state and federal decisions are initially published individually in pamphlets called "slip decisions." Ultimately, they are published chronologically in volumes called "reporters." Published state cases can be located in regional reporters published by West. In addition, some states still publish an official version of state supreme court, and sometimes appellate court, decisions. United States Supreme Court case law is published, in official version, by the federal government in <u>United States Reports</u> ("U.S."). West publishes Supreme Court case law in the <u>Supreme Court Reporter</u> ("S.Ct."). Older cases may also be found, in hardbound copy, in <u>Lawyer's Edition</u> ("L.Ed"), but recent L.Ed case law is now found only on-line. West publishes federal appellate cases in a Federal reporter series ("F.," "F.2d," "F.3d") and Federal district court cases in a supplementary series ("F. Supp."). Very recent state and federal cases from higher courts may be found in <u>United States Law Week</u>.

International Law does not follow the principle of *stare decisis*. However, ICJ case law is very persuasive as a secondary source when arguing a case before the ICJ. ICJ case law may be found at *http://www.un.org/Overview/Organs/icj.html*. For additional sources of International Law as well as information regarding International Law sources, you may want to look to Restatement of the Law, Third, Foreign Relations Law of the United States.

While codified statues can generally be located in the appropriate topical index to the code, statutes published chronologically and case law (which is always published chronologically) are virtually impossible to find without some kind of finding tool. In addition, if the researcher is unfamiliar with the area of law at issue, he or she may not know which statutes are applicable. Thus, the research process may be facilitated by beginning with Secondary Authority.

2. A Short Review of Secondary Authority And Other Finding Tools

a. The Major Sources of Domestic Secondary Authority and other Finding Tools

  i. **Encyclopedias** (Am Jur; C.J.S.)

  - Give you an overview of a topic, but

  - Don't cite; use them as a "finding tool" to locate primary authority

  ii. **Digests**

  - Are a principal way of locating case law because they "link" you to cases published in Reporters by using the West System of key numbers and topic names, but

- Don't cite; use as a "finding tool" to locate primary authority

iii. **Legal Periodicals**

- Are scholarly analyses of legal rules and issues, but
- Don't cite (unless the author is a leader in the field) use as a "finding tool" to locate primary authority

iv. **A.L.R. Annotations**

- Give you a pragmatic, practice-oriented view of legal issues
- Are a good source to locate primary authority
- Do not cite; use as a "finding tool" to locate primary authority

v. **Restatements**

- Are written by scholars and other leaders in a particular field of law
- They distill a consensus view of common law precepts
- They can be cited
- They become primary authority if a jurisdiction adopts

vi. **Uniform Codes and Model Acts**

- Are also drafted by scholars and other experts
- They propose new ways of improving an area of law
- If adopted by the legislature in a jurisdiction, they become primary authority

vii. **Shepards**

- Are not precisely a secondary authority
- They show you prior and subsequent history of primary authority. (E.g., was the case overruled; have other cases cited it; followed it, and so forth)
- They are an invaluable resource for updating primary authority

b. **The Role of Secondary Authority and Other Finding Tools in the Research Process**

> i. They help you find the law (Primary Authority)
> ii They explain the law

That is, they explain a particular **field of law, like** Contracts, Torts or Criminal Law, or they explain **a particular rule of law within a field of law.**

For example, what are the requirements of contract formation? Or what constitutes negligence, or what are the elements of manslaughter? They can also explain **the issue of law ("disputed element") within a particular rule.** For example, does performance of a contract term constitute "acceptance"? Or is there a duty to rescue a person in danger? Or under what circumstances will a self-defense argument exonerate a person of a manslaughter charge?

It is important to note that not all moot court competitions require you to do all of the research process; they may focus on your analytical, writing and oral presentation skills. Nevertheless, when you have completed whatever research is required and located the applicable rule(s) of law, you are ready to prepare an analysis of the problem.

D. Analyzing the Problem; Applying the Applicable Rule of Law to the Relevant Facts of the Case; Developing Theories of the Case

Rules of law are broken down into component parts. These parts may be identified as "elements," "factors," or "prongs." Once you have located the component parts of the applicable rule, then match each part with the facts that are relevant to each part.

Example:

Rule of law = Burglary	Facts
1. breaking	1. Husband ("H") broke a window
2. entry	2. and climbed through it
3. dwelling place	3. into the residence
4. of another	4. he held in joint tenancy with his former wife ("W")
5. in the middle of the night	5. at 1 a.m.

6. with the intent to commit a felony	6. intending to steal her jewels
7. therein	7. from the wall safe

At this point, you will be able to see more precisely what issue or issues are in dispute. Locate precedent case law for each component part of the rule that will be disputed. Mandatory authority, of course, is preferred but you may also use persuasive case law from other jurisdictions in the absence of mandatory precedent. In the facts presented above, element #4 ("of another") is in dispute, because it is not clear whether Husband's joint ownership with another (his former wife) is included in the category "of another." In one sense it is: his former wife is a joint owner. In another sense it isn't: he holds title as well.

Once you have studied the case precedent construing disputed parts of the applicable rule of law, you should develop:

1. A version or interpretation of the applicable rule for your position and a separate one for your opponent's position. For example, if the disputed element in a burglary case were element #4: residency "of another," then:

   H's version of the Rule:

   Burglary penalizes felonious conduct that occurs in residences where the perpetrator has no property interest.

   State's version of the Rule:

   Burglary penalizes felonious conduct that occurs in any residence in which a third person has a property interest.

2. A theory of the case for your position and your opponent's position. Example:

   H's theory of the case:

   H owned the residence as a joint tenant, hence it is not the residence "of another."

   State's theory of the case:

   Because H's former wife had a property interest in the residence as a joint tenant, it was the residence "of another."

Notice that the theory of the case applies a party's version of the applicable rule to his version of the facts. It is thus, a legal syllogism expressed as a thesis statement. The thesis statement is a concise statement of one party's theory of the case. The legal syllogism identifies the applicable law as the major premise; the relevant facts as the minor premise; and the party's position on the issue as the legal conclusion. The legal syllogism is discussed in more detail on page 25.

Now begin to think strategically about developing your argument. Different moot court problems pose different analytical and organizational challenges for the brief writer. What follows are some general guidelines for developing an effective argument:

- If your case is on appeal, you are limited to the issues raised on appeal. Generally, the reviewing court will not hear other issues.

- Select your best arguments and list them in the order of their strength (strongest argument first). Eliminate arguments that seem weak (unpersuasive) or legally irrelevant (they won't really help you win the case).

- Identify your opponent's arguments and rank them according to strength and relevancy. As to each argument, decide whether you will: 1) ignore it (usually the best approach for weak or irrelevant arguments, but also consider ignoring a potentially strong argument if you believe the opponent won't find or develop it); 2) dismiss it summarily; or 3) confront it explicitly and develop a counter-argument (usually a good policy for the opponent's strongest arguments that you are sure will be raised). In any case, if you choose to address any of the opponent's arguments you should always develop your argument on that issue first, before you identify the opponent's argument and show why its flawed.

- Decide what case precedent and what factual evidence (noting the location of each piece of evidence in the record) you will use to support each of your argument.

Now you are ready to construct the brief.

E. Drafting the Brief

1. The Parts of the Brief

Each moot court competition will include a set of rules on formatting and organizing the brief. Excerpts from sample briefs are reprinted in Chapter 2 as representative examples. Full versions of sample briefs for particular Moot Court Competitions can often be found on the Competition's website. For example, the website for the Stetson International Environmental Law Competition is found at *http://www.law.stetson. edu/mootct*. Copies of actual briefs filed with the U.S. Supreme Court are also available on-line. Sample briefs may also be found in your law library. For example, Jessup's International Law Competition publishes winning briefs each year (Phillip C. Jessup International Law Moot Court Competition Compendium published by ASIL annually). And most law school libraries have copies of the annual compendia. Finally, your coach may have copies of competition briefs from prior years. You may use the sample briefs as illustrations of how the rules for formatting and organizing the brief for a particular competition look when applied to a particular legal problem.

You must follow the local rules for your competition meticulously, and the following example is only a typical format. A *typical* format for a moot court brief *may* include:

1. Cover page

    Top left part of page = case caption

    Middle of the page = title of the document

    Lower right part of page = student's name

2. Table of Contents (Index)

    The Table of Contents (sometimes called an Index) identifies each section in the brief and its page number. It also lists under the Argument section, all the point and sub-headings. Therefore, by looking at the Argument section of the Table of Contents, a reader has complete sentence outline of your theory of the case and your arguments.

    Pagination in the brief begins with the Table of Contents. The Table of Contents and the Table of Authorities are numbered in lower case roman numerals. After the Tables, pagination is by arabic numbers.

3. Table of Authorities

    The Table of Authorities is a complete list of all legal authorities used in the brief and the pages on which they appear. The Table of Authorities is broken down into categories: first, list the cases (in alphabetical order); then list statutes and constitutional provisions (or administrative regulations and court rules; if any) in the following order:1) federal Constitution; 2) state Constitutions; 3) federal statutes; 4) state statutes; 5) court rules; 6) federal agency regulations; and 7) state agency regulations; then cite to any <u>legislative history</u> you will use in your brief; and finally include a <u>miscellaneous</u> section for any secondary authority you use in the brief. Secondary authority is cited in the following order: restatements, treatises, law review articles and internet sources.

4. <u>Opinion Below</u>

   If the lower court's opinion has been reported, give its citation; if not, then cite to the page in the Record where it is found.

5. <u>Jurisdiction</u>

   State the specific legal authority — rule or statute — under which the jurisdiction of the appellate court is invoked.

6. <u>Statutes Involved</u>

   Give the citations of the statutes referenced in the Brief and note that the text of each statute is found in the Appendix to the Brief.

7. <u>Preliminary Statement</u>

   Succinctly identify the parties, the nature of the action, procedural history, motion before the court and what you want the court to do. It should advocate (that is, it should attempt to persuade the court) but appear to be objective.

8. <u>Question or Questions Presented</u>

   Identify the issue or issues before the Court. In your first year Legal Analysis and Writing class you were instructed that in drafting the Question and Answer Section of an objective law firm memorandum, each Question and Answer must contain the applicable rule of law (that is, what is the rule of law under which plaintiff's claim or cause of action was brought), the disputed elements (that is, what elements of the applicable rule of law are the focus of the dispute in this case), the facts pivotal to those elements (that is, which facts are most relevant to the resolution of the elements in dispute), and the conclusion or resolution of the dispute you believe a court of law would reach on each Question (the "Answer").

   Example of a Question and Answer Section in a Law Firm Memorandum:

   rule of law
   ↓

   <u>Question:</u>   Did Husband commit the crime of burglary when he

pivotal facts
↓

broke into a house he owned as a joint tenant with his former wife?

legal conclusion
↓

Answer: No. The crime of burglary is only committed upon the breaking and entry into the

disputed element
↓

dwelling place "of another." Husband did not break into the house "of another" but into a residency to which he held title.

Good briefwriting follows the same model, with one exception. In the brief there is no explicit "Answer" but the Question contains the applicable rule, disputed element(s) and pivotal facts; and the persuasive way in which you draft them strongly suggests the "Answer."

Example of a Question Presented Section in an Appellate Brief:

Question Presented:

pivotal facts
↓

Can Husband be convicted of burglarizing a residency he jointly owns when the

rule of law
↓

crime of burglary requires a breaking and entry into the

disputed element
↓

residency "of another"?

Another feature that distinguishes the Questions Presented section in a brief from the kind of "Q & A" section you may be familiar with from drafting law firm memoranda of law in your Legal Analysis and Writing class is that the issues in appellate briefs always include a procedural or "umbrella issue." The "umbrella" issue is the issue which brings the case before the court. For example, in our Burglary Example, suppose the jury convicts Husband of burglary. Then, suppose Husband files a Motion for Acquittal Notwithstanding the Verdict. Assume that the trial court denies the Motion. Husband, then, appeals the trial court's decision and argues that the trial court erred in denying Husband's Motion for Acquittal. Husband's Question Presented on appeal could include the umbrella issue.

Example: *umbrella issue*
                                                    ↓

<u>Question Presented</u>:   Should Husband's Motion to Acquit him of

rule of law
    ↓

burglary be granted

                    pivotal facts
                            ↓

when he broke into a home he owned jointly with his former wife and not into the home

        disputed element
                ↓

"of another"?

When you have an umbrella rule of law, that is, the rule under which the moving party asks the Court to review the case (summary judgment, for example) and a substantive rule, the rule of law under which plaintiff's claim was brought (negligence, for example) both should be included.

    Example:

                                    umbrella rule
                                            ↓

Should a landowner be granted a preliminary injunction against a neighbor's

                    pivotal facts
                            ↓

front yard display of thirty-six, lighted 5 feet tall bunny rabbits when the

                disputed element of substantive rule
                                    ↓

display does not interfere with the landowner's reasonable enjoyment

                disputed element of umbrella rule
                                    ↓

of his property and he is, therefore, unlikely to succeed on the merits

substantive rule
↓
of his nuisance suit against the neighbor?

9. Statement of the Case (or Facts)

The statement of the case is typically a chronological recitation of the facts which are stated in a way that is favorable to your client's position without distorting the facts. Beginning on page 28, below, you are given detailed instructions on how to draft facts "persuasively."

In an appellate brief, you must cite to the record for any facts you include. The citations should be placed in parenthesis and may appear in this form: (R. at _____). Check your local rules for the citation form that you are required to use when citing to the record.

10. Summary of the Argument

A brief statement, generally no longer than a paragraph for each major issue, as to why your client should prevail. Include enough pivotal facts to make your summary persuasive.

11. Argument

The Argument section is the section in which you develop your analysis of the legal problem at issue. If you were required to draft an objective law firm memorandum in a Legal Writing and Analysis class, you may recall that the Argument section in the Memorandum calls for an analysis which presents and weighs the merits of the argument that can be made on both sides of the issue and then predicts which side will prevail. The Argument section in an appellate brief is distinguishable from the Argument section in an objective Memorandum because its purpose is to advocate one side of the case. It is drafted to advocate your theory of the case rather than to weigh the merits of each side's argument as you may have done in the objective law firm memorandum.

The Argument in an appellate brief uses point headings and subheadings to focus and to lead the reader's mind through the Argument. These point headings and subheadings form a complete sentence-by-sentence outline of your theory of the case. Each point heading is a separate and complete ground for you to prevail on the legal issue identified in the point heading.

EXAMPLE OF A POINT HEADING

THE BURGLARY INDICTMENT OF HUSBAND MUST BE DISMISSED BECAUSE HE OWNED THE RESIDENCY HE BROKE

INTO AS A JOINT TENANT; HENCE IT WAS NOT THE HOME "OF ANOTHER."

A detailed explanation of headings begins on page 18; more information about the Argument Section appears on pages 25–27.

12. Conclusion

Begin with a conclusion on the substantive issue (example: "Husband cannot be convicted of burglary"). Then include one to three sentences explaining your conclusion and summarizing your legal analysis of the disputed sub-issues (example: "The residence into which he broke and entered was not the home 'of another' for purposes of the crime of burglary because he owned it jointly with his former wife"). Then finish with one sentence summarizing the relief you are praying for on the umbrella issue (example: "Therefore the indictment must be dismissed"). More information about the Conclusion section is given on page 32.

13. Endorsement

Sign the brief as indicated in the "local rules." The format typically includes:

"Respectfully submitted," then, under your signature line:

your name

the party you represent

phone number and the law school address

(example: see, *http://www.legalnet.law.stetson.edu*)

14. Appendix

The Appendix contains the relevant texts of the statutes cited in the brief.

Now that we have identified the sections of the brief, you are ready to draft each section.

2. Developing Each Part of the Brief

Each analytical part of the brief should be written persuasively. Now that you have completed your analysis of the legal problem, developed a version of the rule and a theory of the case for your argument and for your opponent's argument, identified legal authority (especially case law) in support of each argument and reviewed the format and its component parts, you should begin to draft the brief.

Begin with the Point Headings and Sub-Headings

Point Headings

Each Point Heading (sometimes called a "contention") identifies a separate ground for relief. It should:

- Be a complete sentence, in capital letters, single-spaced (and in the text of the argument, it should be centered in the page);

- Be an affirmative statement expressed in the active voice;

- Be a persuasive statement of your argument on the issue which includes or alludes to: the applicable law, the part of the law that is in dispute, the legal conclusion you want the Court to reach on the dispute and facts pivotal to that resolution; and yet

- Be stated as concisely, simply and directly as possible

For example:

legal conclusion
↓
A HUSBAND CANNOT BE CONVICTED OF

rule of law
↓
BURGLARIZING THE RESIDENCE HE

pivotal facts
↓
HOLDS IN JOINT TENANCY WITH HIS EX-WIFE BECAUSE IT IS NOT

disputed element
↓
THE HOME "OF ANOTHER."

Because the issue is before the Court on a procedural ("umbrella") issue the first Point Heading should allude to and reach a conclusion about the umbrella issue. In the next example, assume that an employee has sued his employer under a state common law Tort of Outrage. Assume, further, that the elements of the Tort are:

1) Any person or entity

2) who intentionally or recklessly

3) engages in extreme or outrageous conduct

4) which causes another

5) severe emotional distress

6) is liable for the damages

In response to Employee's Motion for Summary Judgment on his claim against his Employer, the Employer's first Point Heading might be:

legal conclusion   *umbrella issue*
    ↓   ↓

AN EMPLOYEE IS NOT ENTITLED TO JUDGMENT AS A

substantive rule of law
↓

MATTER OF LAW FOR HIS TORT OF OUTRAGE CLAIM AGAINST HIS EMPLOYER

BECAUSE THE EMPLOYER'S REINSTATEMENT CONDITIONS IN

pivotal facts
↓

REQUIRING EMPLOYEE TO APOLOGIZE WERE NOT

disputed element and conclusion
↓

OUTRAGEOUS BUT CONSTITUTED REASONABLE ATTEMPTS TO RESTORE AN AMICABLE WORK ENVIRONMENT FOR ITS EMPLOYEES.

Notice in the next example of <u>Employee v. Employer</u> only Point Headings are used because each issue is relatively simple. There is no need to subdivide the analysis of each contention. Notice each Point-Heading addresses a separate and independent ground for relief on an issue: I and II address the separate grounds for relief on the substantive issue of the tort of outrage; III addresses the separate issue of compensatory damages; and IV addresses punitive damages. Notice the order in which the Point Headings are presented. Point Headings I and II would give Employer complete relief (no liability) while III and IV, even though they are separate and independent grounds for relief, would only give the Employer partial relief (reduction in the damage award). Point Headings I and II are the preferred remedies (because they give Employer complete relief); therefore they precede III and IV.

Example:

<u>POINT-HEADINGS</u> (in descending order of preference)

<u>Employee v. Employer</u>

umbrella issue
↓

I. SUMMARY JUDGMENT IN FAVOR OF EMPLOYEE'S

substantive rule   *conclusion*
↓   ↓

TORT OF OUTRAGE SUIT SHOULD BE VACATED
WHERE EMPLOYER'S EVIDENCE DISPUTES

                          disputed element
                          ↓

EMPLOYEE'S CLAIM THAT IT ENGAGED IN OUTRAGEOUS

                  pivotal facts
                  ↓

CONDUCT AND SHOWS EMPLOYER MERELY AT-
TEMPTED TO FOSTER A RECONCILIATION BETWEEN
EMPLOYEE AND A MANAGER BY REQUIRING EM-
PLOYEE TO APOLOGIZE.

         umbrella issue and conclusion
         ↓

II. SUMMARY JUDGMENT SHOULD HAVE BEEN
    DENIED BECAUSE A JURY COULD HAVE FOUND THE

                          disputed element
                          ↓

EMPLOYEE'S EMOTIONAL DISTRESS WAS CAUSED

              pivotal facts
              ↓

BY A MANAGER'S MISCONDUCT AND NOT BY EM-
PLOYER'S LEGITIMATE BUSINESS EFFORTS TO DIFFUSE
EMPLOYEE'S ANIMOSITY TOWARD THE MANAGER.

III. THE TRIAL COURT'S AWARD OF COMPENSATORY DAM-
     AGES IN THE SUM OF $2.3 MILLION WAS EXCESSIVE
     AND MUST BE REDUCED.

IV. AN AWARD OF PUNITIVE DAMAGES WAS ERROR AS A
    MATTER OF LAW.

Organization of Point Headings: (Reviewed):

If there is a threshold or umbrella or procedural issue it should be included in the contention on any substantive issue to which it applies. For example, in a case where an injured patient sues a doctor for medical malpractice and the Doctor moves for Dismissal of the lawsuit, the Patient's first Point Headings should begin: "DOCTOR'S MOTION TO DISMISS PATIENT'S CLAIM FOR MEDICAL MALPRACTICE MUST BE DENIED BECAUSE...

Then, always rank your Point-Headings (contentions) in order of their strength and their ability to obtain maximum relief for your client. Sometimes, even if a party has a strong legal argument in support of a contention, it may not be ranked highly because it does not give the party maximum relief. In the preceding example of Employee v. Employer, the Employer may have a strong argument against punitive damages. But because denial of punitives gives the employer only partial relief, the contentions regarding the substantive claim (the tort of outrage) come first because if the claim is dismissed on either ground the Employer gets the maximum relief it seeks.

Sub-Headings

As the name suggests, sub-headings develop parts or sub-divisions of the major contention in more detail. The number of sub-headings you use reflects the complexity of your argument. Do not make your argument draconian by using more sub-headings than you need to lead the reader through your argument. Do not use sub-headings if the analysis does not lend itself easily to sub-division. Sub-headings are typed in lower case (like regular sentences in the text) and they are underlined.

POINT-HEADINGS AND SUB-HEADINGS

In the following examples, notice how the Point Headings and Sub-Headings form a sentence outline of the party's legal argument.

More Examples

In the next example, a dealership asserts a claim against an automobile manufacturer under the Automobile Dealers Day in Court Act, 15 U.S.C.A. § 1221, et seq., which provides, in pertinent part, that a dealer may bring suit against a manufacturer with which it has a franchise agreement, on the grounds that the manufacturer failed to act in good faith in one or more of the following respects:

1) in operating under the provisions of the agreement or

2) in terminating it,

3) canceling it,

4) or refusing to renew it.

In the hypothetical below, Dealership argues Manufacturer violated the Act when it: (1) failed to reimburse Dealer for valid warranty claims; (2) demanded that Dealer relocate to a less-promising market location as a precondition for renewing its franchise; and (3) tried to coerce Dealer into raising its prices above competitive levels as a precondition for supplying Dealer with the models it ordered. At trial, Dealer argued these actions contravened Manufacturer's good faith obligations under the Act. If the trial court granted Manufacturer's Motion for Summary Judgment, then when Dealer appeals, the contentions in its brief might be organized in Point Headings and Sub-Headings as follows:

Dealership v. Manufacturer

I. SUMMARY JUDGMENT MUST BE VACATED AND THE CASE REMANDED FOR TRIAL WHERE DEALER CAN SHOW THAT MANUFACTURER BREACHED THE PROVISIONS OF THE FRANCHISE AGREEMENT BY FAILING TO REIMBURSE WARRANTY CLAIMS COVERED BY THE EXPRESS TERMS OF THE AGREEMENT, THEREBY VIOLATING THE DUTY OF GOOD FAITH MANDATED BY THE AUTOMOBILE DEALER'S DAY IN COURT ACT.

A. Failure to comply with the express terms of the Franchise requiring credit to Dealer for covered warranty services performed by Dealer is bad faith.

B. Whether delays in excess of two years in warranty reimbursements constitutes lack of good faith is an issue of fact for the jury.

C. Refusal to credit dealer claims identical to those of other dealers in the vicinity which Manufacturer did honor is unfair and violates Manufacturer's obligation of good faith.

II. THE TRIAL COURT ERRED BY RULING, AS A MATTER OF LAW, THAT MANUFACTURER DID NOT BREACH ITS DUTY OF GOOD FAITH WHEN

IT CONDITIONED RENEWAL OF THE FRAN-
CHISE ON DEALER'S AGREEMENT TO MOVE TO
A COMMERCIALLY UNDESIRABLE LOCATION.

A. When the evidence is disputed as to whether a particular locale is commercially viable then a jury
should resolve the issue.

B. The presence of an established competitor in the
locale is relevant to the issue of Dealer's potential
market share and should be considered by a jury.

III. COMPELLING DEALER TO RAISE ITS PRICES AS A
PRECONDITION FOR RECEIVING ITS PROPOR-
TIONATE SHARE OF MANUFACTURER'S VEHI-
CLES IS COERCIVE BEHAVIOR WHICH IS BAD
FAITH, PER SE, UNDER THE DEALERSHIP'S DAY
IN COURT ACT; THEREFORE SUMMARY JUDG-
MENT IN FAVOR OF MANUFACTURER WAS IN-
APPROPRIATE.

Another Hypothetical

Sometimes court opinions from the "real world" effectively illustrate
how complex issues can be persuasively organized by appropriate headings. In a recent case, Made in the USA Foundation v. U.S., 2001 WL
194857 (11th Cir. 2001), a labor union and other parties sued the federal government alleging that NAFTA's "fast track" provision violates
the Treaty Clause, Article II, Section 2, of the Constitution. The Treaty
Clause circumscribes the President's treaty-making power by requiring
Senate approval. Specifically, the Clause accords the President, "the
power, by and with the advice and consent of the Senate, to make
treaties, provided two-thirds of the Senators present concur." By contrast, under NAFTA's Implementation Act, only a simple majority affirmative vote of both Houses is required.

Assume for purposes of our hypothetical case, which we'll identify as
Labor Union v. U.S., that the Government asserted that the plaintiffs
lacked standing to sue and that, in any case, the issue was not justiciable because it was a political question. Assume, further, that at trial the
federal district court found for the plaintiffs (Labor Union, et al.) on the
threshold issue of standing, but agreed with the Government on the
merits. Assume the plaintiffs appeal the district court's summary judgment in favor of the Government to the appropriate federal circuit
court. There, the plaintiff-appellants (Labor Union, et al.) argue that:

1) the decision of the federal district court on the threshold standing issue (that the plaintiffs had standing) should be affirmed, but

2) its ruling on the merits (that the issue was a nonjusticiable question) should be reversed and remanded. Obviously, Labor Union's argument on the merits is that NAFTA's implementation was unconstitutional: that Congressional approval of NAFTA by simple majority was in contravention of the Constitutionally mandated two-thirds of the Senate approval which, thereby, renders NAFTA's Implementation Act void.

In response, Government has two separate and independent grounds for relief. It can reiterate both its "standing" argument (plaintiffs lack standing) and its "political question" argument (the issue poses a "political question" and, therefore, is not justiciable). Therefore, the Argument in Government's Appellate Brief can be organized under two Point Headings. Furthermore, each of these contentions lends itself easily to sub-headings and, in at least one instance, to sub-sub headings. The headings might be crafted as follows:

I. THIS COURT SHOULD REVERSE THE DISTRICT COURT'S HOLDING THAT LABOR UNION HAD STANDING TO CHALLENGE THE CONSTITUTIONALITY OF NAFTA'S IMPLEMENTATION BECAUSE LABOR UNION CANNOT SHOW IT SUFFERED ACTUAL INJURY TRACEABLE TO NAFTA WHICH IS LIKELY TO BE REDRESSED BY A RULING THAT NAFTA IS VOID.

   A. Labor Union is unable to show that it has suffered "injury in fact."

      1. Labor Union's testimonial evidence of deterioration in working conditions and employee compensation is neither concrete nor particularized.

      2. Labor Union's contention that U.S. labor standards will be subverted by NAFTA is merely conjectural.

   B. There is no persuasive evidence on the record that any diminution in employment conditions has been caused by the implementation of NAFTA.

C. The Labor Union has failed to demonstrate that termination of U.S. participation in NAFTA will alleviate the conditions of which it complains.

II. BECAUSE THE CONSTITUTION HAS RELEGATED ISSUES OF FOREIGN AND INTERNATIONAL COMMERCE TO THE EXECUTIVE AND LEGISLA-TIVE BRANCHES, THE CLAIM FILED BY LABOR UNION IMPLICATES A NONJUSTICIABLE POLITI-CAL QUESTION WHICH MUST BE DISMISSED.

A. The Constitution has entrusted foreign commerce issues, the subject-matter of NAFTA, to the political branches of government.

B. The issues raised by labor union's claims are beyond the jurisdictional purview and expertise of the judiciary.

C. The need for uniformity and considerations of prudence dictate that the judiciary refrain from intervening.

After you have organized your argument by drafting the headings you are ready to draft the text of the Argument section.

Argument

Now that you have an outline of your argument (Point-Headings and Sub-Headings) you are ready to develop each contention and sub-contention. The organizational model most often employed for developing contentions in a legal brief is an embellished version of the legal syllogism. Recall that the syllogism is the form that deductive reasoning takes in the legal culture because of its appearance of objectivity. The major premise (the pertinent rule of law) is applied to the minor premise (the relevant facts) in the case to reach a legal conclusion.

Notice in the outline of the expanded legal syllogism that follows, the syllogism is embellished by cases that explain or define terms in the Rule and the syllogism is supported or "proved" by case law analogy.

LEGAL SYLLOGISM

Major Premise (rule of law):   All men are mortal.

    rule explanation: 1)   Courts have defined the term "mortal" to mean, "you die, fool." (string cites with signals and parentheticals)

2) The Supreme Court held that the term "men" must include "women" for both Constitutional law and natural law purposes. (cite)

rule-narrowing: In this case, the term "mortal" is not disputed. Only the class covered by "men" is in dispute.

Minor Premise: Socrates was a man. (Case facts)

fact analogies: 1) Brutus wore a toga and it was held in Brutus v. Caesar that Brutus was a man. (cite) Socrates also wore a toga and the fact that he didn't know Caesar is not relevant. Therefore Socrates was a man.

2) Plato was a philosopher and he was found to be a man. (cite) Socrates was a philosopher, so he must be a man.

Legal Conclusion: Socrates was mortal because he was a man.

Notice how the classic syllogism: major premise: All men are mortal

minor premise: Socrates was a man

conclusion: Therefore Socrates was mortal

is embellished and supported (or "proved") by case law analogy. The deductive reasoning of the syllogism is often used as a strategic devise of persuasion in brief writing, because it appears to be objective. Now, if you insert legal syllogisms (expanded by case law analogies) into your analysis, your Argument section of the brief might follow this organizational structure:

MACRO-ORGANIZATION OF IDEAS IN THE SYLLOGISM FORMAT

Point Heading

I. Introductory Paragraph or Paragraphs

A. Persuasively state the issue the court will address.

B. Reach an overall conclusion about the procedural motion or umbrella issues and include a concise explanation for your overall ultimate conclusion (syllogism).

C. Identify the applicable rule of law for the umbrella issue.

Paraphrase it, quote it and/or identify its elements in a way that is favorable to your client. Cite.

D. Narrow the reader's focus and forecast your argument by:

1. Explaining what the rule means—cite—and/or
2. Explaining its purpose/policy—cite—and/or
3. Explaining what elements are in dispute and/or
4. Identifying relevant burdens of proof and standards of review—cite.

E. Summarize the facts in a way that is favorable to your position on the umbrella issue.

F. Reach a conclusion as to how the umbrella issue applies to each of the arguments you will raise on the substantive issue.

G. At your option take a preemptive strike at your opponent's theory of the case.

II. <u>Analysis</u>

<u>First Sub-Heading</u>

A. As to each argument you will make on each issue, begin with a conclusory statement as to why you should prevail on this particular ground or basis. Include pivotal facts.

B. Identify and cite the applicable rule persuasively.

C. Explain the rule to narrow the reader's focus and cite to authority which validates your explanation.

D. Apply your version of the rule (major premise) to the facts in the case (minor premise) and reach a conclusion.

E. Prove your syllogism with case law analogies.
   (Note: Because this is persuasive writing you may or may not want to argue both sides of the analogy.)

F. One sentence conclusion on the issue.

<u>Second Sub-Heading</u>

Same drill for each issue (argument) you will raise.

Now you have completed your argument. The next section you should draft is the Statement of the Case. Preparing the Statement of the Case after you prepare your Argument helps to insure that you include all the facts you use to develop your Argument in the Statement of the Case. It is crucial that all the facts that appear in the Argument Section also appear in the Statement of the Case.

The Statement of Case (Facts)

The Statement of Case should include the pre-litigation facts that gave rise to the legal action and the procedural history of the case. It should include an introductory statement and a concluding statement.

While there is no single approach to organizing the facts, consider the guidelines that follow. For purposes of these guidelines, we will use a case in which the defendant appeals a death sentence imposed upon him for a murder he committed when he was 15 years old. This example is modeled on an actual case, Thompson v. Oklahoma, 487 U.S. 815, 108 S.Ct. 2682, 101 L.Ed.2d 707 (1988). The defendant's theory of the case is that capital punishment for a crime committed by a 15 year old is "cruel and unusual" and, therefore, unconstitutional under the Eighth Amendment because a 15 year old is too immature to appreciate the full implications of his misconduct.

His statement of the case should reflect that theory. It should begin with an introductory paragraph identifying the parties and the nature of the action. It should do so in a way that: (1) gives the reader the "big picture" of the case; (2) implicitly favors the client; and (3) expresses his theory of the case.

Example of an Introductory Paragraph

When William Wayne Thompson was only fifteen years old he participated in the murder of his brother-in-law. William Wayne and his adult co-defendants were subsequently convicted of first degree murder and sentenced to die. On appeal, the issue is whether William Wayne was so young at the time of his offense that he lacked the maturity fully to appreciate the wrongfulness of his involvement.

Then recite the pre-litigation facts

The pre-litigation facts are generally presented in chronological order; however a topical order (facts relevant to each legal issue) can also be effective, especially in legally complex cases. The pre-litigation facts must include all relevant facts: facts relevant to any legal issue raised by the argument and unfavorable facts as well as facts favorable to your client's perspective. One technique for drafting persuasive facts is to generalize unfavorable facts and state favorable facts with specificity.

Make sure you stick to the record. That means two things:

- Generally, use only facts found within the four corners of the record. Be very careful not to present inferences as facts. If you do include an inference, delineate it as such and make sure it is an eminently reasonable one.

- Identify the place in the record where the fact can be found. Use the parenthetical cite described earlier.

Make sure that you are discussing facts, not legal conclusions or legal characterization of the facts. Do not say, "Mr. Brown was negligent." Just say, "He ran a red light." Don't cite to the law in the fact statement. Don't use pejorative language: your opponent is not a "jerk" (well, maybe he is, but...). In addition to legally relevant facts, include enough background facts to make the narrative interesting and easy to understand. After you have covered the pre-litigation facts, recite the procedural history of the case. Then your concluding statement should identify the posture of the case: the motion that brings the case to the court's attention now.

Example of Statement of Facts

(A Revision of the Majority's Statement
in Thompson v. Oklahoma)

Introduction

When William Wayne Thompson was only fifteen years old he participated in the murder of his brother-in-law. William Wayne and his adult co-defendants were subsequently convicted of first degree murder and sentenced to die. On appeal, the issue is whether William Wayne was so young at the time of the offense that he lacked the maturity fully to appreciate the wrongfulness of his involvement.

Pre-Litigation Facts

In the early morning hours of January 23, 1983, William Wayne's brother-in-law died of knife and firearm injuries, as well as physical blows, inflicted upon him by three adult males and William Wayne. It is undisputed that the assault which killed William Wayne's brother-in-law was planned, that William Wayne was aware of the plan, that he told three older friends and his girlfriend about the plan and that William Wayne participated in the assault which resulted in his brother-in-law's death. The evidence shows that after the assault, William Wayne participated in throwing the body in the Washita River with a concrete block attached to it.

It is also undisputed that the brother-in-law had physically abused William Wayne's sister and that, following the incident, William Wayne told his mother that the brother-in-law was dead and his sister, Vicki, "wouldn't have to worry about him any more." At the time of the offense William Wayne was, as a fifteen year old, considered to be a "child" under the law of the State of Oklahoma where he was tried, convicted and sentenced to die.

Procedural History   His legal status as a child required a pretrial hearing on his competency to stand trial as an adult for acts committed while he was a minor. Following the hearing, the trial court certified William Wayne to stand trial as an adult. During both the guilt phase and the penalty phase of the trial, the prosecutor introduced color photographs which graphically showed the condition of the decedent brother-in-law's body after it was removed from the river. On appeal, the Court of Criminal Appeals held that use of the photographs during the guilt phase while error, was harmless error. The Court did not consider whether use of the photos during the penalty phase was error.

During the penalty phase, the jury found that the murder was cruel. However, the jury also found that William Wayne was unlikely to commit criminal acts of violence in the future. The Court of Criminal Appeals affirmed the jury's conviction and sentence justifying its opinion on the grounds that if a defendant is certified to be tried as an adult it is Constitutionally permissible for him to be punished as an adult.

Concluding Statement William Wayne Thompson appeals the lower court's evidentiary ruling and the sentence it imposed. He argues that the sentence must be set aside.

In this example, the briefwriter must concede the brutality of the murder but tries to refocus the reader's attention on facts that emphasize Thompson's youth and immaturity and his probable motive: defending his sister from an abusive spouse. Notice, for example, that the briefwriter consistently describes Thompson as acting only in concert with adult defendants and as reporting to adults both before and after the murder. The use of Thompson's given names also seems to emphasize his youth.

One final point. In our example we have omitted citations to the Record. but make sure that when you draft your Statement of the Case you include appropriate cites pursuant to the citation form required by the Competition's "local rules." Once you have completed your Statement of the Case, the next section you should draft is the Conclusion. The Conclusion is a very concise recapitulation of everything that you advocated in your Argument Section.

The Conclusion

Begin by stating the conclusion you want the court to reach. State it persuasively. For example "The Employer is not entitled to summary judgment because the Employee has made out a prima facie case on her sexual harassment claim." Then, summarize your argument on each disputed element or issue of the substantive issue. In this example, show the employee can establish a prima facie case on her sexual harassment claim: some probative evidence on each element of the claim. Conclude by stating the relief you seek, exactly what you want the Court to do: "Therefore, Employer's Motion for Summary Judgment must be denied." Always make sure that your last sentence in the Conclusion reiterates the precise relief you want the Court to grant.

Once you have completed drafts of the Headings, Argument, Statement of the Case and Conclusion you are ready to draft the Questions Presented Section.

The Question or Questions Presented

These are the major issues before the Court. There is some latitude on the number of major issues you believe the court must address. Your contentions (Point Headings) have already resolved that problem. Now simply redraft the Point Headings as issues rather than as contentions. State them persuasively by including enough facts to lead the reader to the resolution you seek.

You can select one of two formats:

- The "whether" format: For example:

  Whether imposition of a death sentence on an individual who commits a capital offense when he is 15 years violates the Eighth Amendment's prohibition of cruel and unusual punishment because a minor is too immature to appreciate the full implications of his actions.

  or

- The "is...when (or because)" format: For example:

  Is imposition of a death sentence for a crime committed by a 15 year old cruel and unusual punishment under the Eighth Amendment because a minor is too immature to appreciate the implications of his misconduct?

Now you have drafted the major components of the brief and you are ready to complete the brief by composing short statements for the following sections:

The Preliminary Statement; Opinion Below; Jurisdictional Statement; Statutes Involved and Summary of the Argument.

These sections were previously described on pages 12–17.

> The Bells and Whistles:
>
> Cover Page
>
> Table of Contents
>
> Table of Authorities
>
> Appendix

These sections were also previously described on pages 12–17.

Now that you have completed the brief, review it to make sure you have observed the following rules.

3. Stylistic Conventions

Basic guidelines to remember are:

- Use the active voice unless you have a strategic reason for using passive voice.

- Either call the parties by their proper names or select a legal role that is relevant to the issue before the Court (example: if it is a lease issue, don't call the parties "Appellant" and "Appellee" call them "Landlord" and "Tenant").

- Avoid long quotations. Paraphrase and cite instead. Quotations interfere with the logical flow of your argument.

- Use topic sentences and transition words to tie your paragraphs together in a logical progression.

- Remember: long sentences are used to describe; short sentences are used to convey a sense of judgment. (examples: "The motion should be denied."; "That case is inapposite."; "Defendant's proposition is unsupported.")

- Lead the court systemically through the reasoning process you want her to follow.

- Don't hesitate to argue in the alternative: to give the court optional grounds for ruling in your favor.

- Generally, distinguish unfavorable authority on the facts rather than criticizing it as "poorly reasoned." Judges are sensitive about "trashing" their colleagues.

Finally, review your brief to insure that your facts and legal authority are properly cited.

4. Citation

Check the local rules to see which citation rules you should follow. Generally, the Bluebook's "Practitioner" rules are required but some competitions call for ALWD as a citation resource.

In Chapter 2, we illustrate these concepts with excerpts from sample briefs.

Chapter 2

Examples of Briefs

With the expansion of electronic databases and the internet, there are a number of sources for students to locate examples of briefs. As discussed in Chapter 1, several competitions now put briefs online. In addition, some competitions reprint winning briefs in book form or in law reviews. You should check these sources for copies of briefs from prior years. And don't forget to check with your coach and with any student appellate advocacy board at your school. They might also have copies of briefs from previous competitions. Finally, Westlaw and Lexis both contain copies of briefs filed with the United States Supreme Court.

Given this wealth of resources, we have opted not to reprint a brief in its entirety. Instead, what follows are sample excerpts from the argument section of two briefs, one good and one bad. The excerpts are presented with annotations to bring your attention to specific techniques found in each brief. But before we present the excerpts, a word about the scoring of the brief.

A. Scoring the Brief

As mentioned in Chapter 1, you *must* carefully read the rules of each competition regarding the format and structure of the brief. The competition rules should also give you some guidance as to how the brief score will be factored in to each round's score. What the rules might not be explicit about, however, are the actual grading criteria. Some competitions list these criteria in the rules, but many others do not. Regardless of whether the rules list the judge's scoring criteria, most competitions use a similar set of factors, and these factors are not much different from those used by legal writing professors:

- Format
- Style and Grammar

- Organization
- Strength of Argument
- Use of Authority
- Anticipation of/Method of Dealing With Opponent's Arguments

Within each of these categories, judges are looking for the following:

Format. Does the brief follow the competition rules? These will often include things such as page limits, table of contents, table of authorities, questions presented, and all the other categories discussed in Chapter 1. Following the rules can count for as much as twenty percent of your score, so it is a quick and easy way to accumulate points (and a silly way to lose them). The key here is to know the rules in advance, so that you can follow them as you write, and to make sure you finish the brief with enough time to spare for all the finishing touches and double checks. You should allow at least a week for this final polishing. It definitely *cannot* be completed accurately the night before the brief is due.

Style and Grammar. Does the brief follow standard rules of English? A sloppily written brief conveys a poor message to the judges, undercutting your arguments. It will often have such a strong (although often subconscious) negative effect that it can reduce your points across the board, and not just in this one category.

Organization. Does the brief, especially the argument portion, have a logical flow? Does it conform to appellate brief conventions? (All those things are discussed in Chapter 1, including, for example, point headings and capitalization.) Your brief should walk the reader through the entire argument from start to finish. You don't want the reader to have to stop to think about what you are arguing or to go back and re-read a paragraph to try to decipher what you mean. It should all flow naturally and logically.

Strength of Argument. Once the judges have assessed the format, style, and organization of your argument, they will turn to the substance of that argument. How strong is it? Have you constructed the best possible argument for your client, given the state of existing law? If you have scored well on the previous categories, that will help boost your score here, as the judges will be favorably disposed to your writing. If you have not done well on the prior elements, however, that may hurt your score here, as the judges have already formed an impression of a sloppy brief.

Use of Authority. How well have you used existing authority? Have you drawn accurate conclusions from the cases? Are your citations accurate? Have you used excessive footnotes or string citations? (These are both Bad Things.) Have you used citation where appropriate? Inappropriate? Have you missed any important statutes or cases?

Anticipation of/Method of Dealing With Opponent's Arguments. How well have you anticipated the arguments for the opposing party? Have you adequately dealt with those arguments in your brief? You don't necessarily want to make the other side's arguments for them, but you should know what those arguments will be so that you can structure your arguments in an effective manner, in a way that forecloses or at least minimizes holes in your client's case. In addition, this category will often include an examination of how well you have handled negative authority—those opinions that may undermine your position or your arguments.

B. Excerpts from Sample Briefs

What follows are excerpts from both a good and bad brief on the same issue, one of the issues from the 2001 National Native American Law Students Association Moot Court Competition. The example of a good brief is an excerpt from an actual brief. The example of a bad brief is not an actual student brief; rather, it is an amalgamation of typical student mistakes.

Before we set out the excerpts, however, we should first summarize the factual background of the litigation, which involved the mythical Confederated Tribes of the Columbia River. A hundred years ago, the United States negotiated a treaty with the Confederated Tribes. In return for several million acres of land, the Confederated Tribes secured a promise that they could fish at all "usual and accustomed places" in perpetuity. Fish, and most particularly salmon, play a very large role in the social and religious life of the members of the Confederated Tribes. Under the facts of the problem, however, key species of fish have recently been listed as Endangered, which triggered a duty by two federal agencies, the National Marine Fisheries Service and the U.S. Forest Service, to create a plan to preserve those species of fish. As part of that plan, the federal agencies imposed a ten year moratorium on all fishing, including tribal fishing. The Confederated Tribes filed suit, alleging, among other things, that the moratorium violated the Tribes' treaty fishing rights. Thus, the first issue in the litigation was whether the Endangered Species Act (ESA) abrogated those fishing rights. The District

Court granted summary judgment in favor of the U.S. government, and the Ninth Circuit affirmed. The U.S. Supreme Court granted certiorari, and the student competitors were instructed to prepare a brief to file with the Supreme Court and prepare an oral argument.

The briefs are set out in the larger column, with our annotations added in the left hand column.

1. Excerpt from a Good Brief

This excerpt was drawn from the brief written by Heather White-Man Runs Him and Natalie Landreth of Harvard University Law School. The brief won third place at the 2001 National NALSA Moot Court Competition. The brief was filed on behalf of the petitioners, the Confederated Tribes.

We suggest you first read all the headings and note how they set out the steps in the argument, moving in a clear, logical fashion. Next, read the text of the excerpt from start to finish. Finally, read the text again, but this time also pause to read the annotations we have supplied.

ARGUMENT

Note how the major heading previews both the legal standard and the conclusion the judges are asked to reach.

I. DO THE CONFEDERATED TRIBES RETAIN THEIR TREATY-RESERVED FISHING RIGHTS WHEN THE ENDANGERED SPECIES ACT DOES NOT EXPLICITLY ABROGATE OR EVEN MENTION INDIAN TREATY RIGHTS, AND THERE IS NO LEGISLATIVE HISTORY SUGGESTING THAT INDIAN TREATY RIGHTS WERE MEANT TO BE ABROGATED?

A. The ESA Does Not Automatically Apply To Indian Tribes.

Note the structure of this opening paragraph — brief conclusion, statement of relevant law, short analysis, and the conclusion repeated. It

Indian treaty rights were not automatically abrogated just by the passage of the ESA. There is a presumption that laws of general applicability apply to Indians with quickly disposes of a possible argument and sets the stage for the true issue.

equal force, with three exceptions: 1) the law touches exclusive rights of tribal self-governance in purely intramural matters; 2) the law's application would abrogate rights guaranteed by treaties; and 3) there is proof that Congress did not intend that the law apply to Indians. *United States v. Baker*, 63 F.3d 1478, 1485 (9th Cir. 1995). The ESA falls under the second and third exceptions. Therefore, the Confederated Tribes' treaty rights were not affected simply by the passage of a generally applicable law.

B. Congress Did Not Explicitly State That The ESA Abrogates Or Was Intended To Abrogate Indian Treaty Rights.

Note the clear statement of the relevant legal standard, with citations after each point, but no string cites. You should always lead with the legal standard. Also note the use of clear, short sentences that are easy to follow; this is not a piece of literature — avoid com-

The Confederated Tribes reserved their rights to "take fish at all usual and accustomed locations" in the Treaty of 1855. Unfortunately, Congress can abrogate treaties at will. *Lone Wolf v. Hitchcock*, 187 U.S. 553 (1903). However, the intent to abrogate Indian treaties must be made

plex sentences and fancy words.

clear and plain. *United States v. Santa Fe Pacific Railroad Co.*, 314 U.S. 339, 353 (1941). In the absence of explicit statutory language, the Court has been "extremely reluctant to find congressional abrogation of treaty rights." *Washington v. Washington Commercial Passenger Fishing Vessel Assn.*, 443 U.S. 658, 690 (1979). Treaty abrogation cannot simply be inferred. *Menominee Tribe v. United States*, 391 U.S. 404 (1968). As the Court so succinctly stated in *United States v. Dion*, "Indian treaty rights are too fundamental to be easily cast aside." *Id.*, 476 U.S. 734, 739 (1986). Because of the importance of Indian treaty rights, the intent to abrogate them should be clear.

Excellent anticipation and refutation of likely argument by respondents.

The ESA does not state that it abrogates Indian treaty rights. The ESA does not even mention Indian treaty rights. With the exception of the inclusion of "Indian" in the definition of a person, the ESA is completely silent as to Indians. It cannot be maintained that the ESA explicitly abrogates treaty rights. Moreover, in the absence of an explicit statement, the Court should be extremely reluctant to find them abrogated.

Clear, easy to read heading—not too wordy.

C. **There Is No Evidence In The Legislative History Of The ESA That Congress Considered Or Intended To Abrogate Indian Treaty-Reserved Rights.**

Again, leading with statement of law. Note how brief avoids explaining all possibly relevant law at the beginning, but rather breaks it into logical steps and interposes relevant analysis and point headings.

The Court has not restricted itself to requiring an explicit statement of intent to abrogate on the face of the act. Abrogation can also be established if the "surrounding circumstances and legislative history" show that Congress intended to abrogate Indian treaty rights. *Mattz v. Arnett*, 412 U.S. 481, 505 (1973); *Rosebud Sioux Tribe v. Kneip*, 430 U.S. 584 (1977) ("In other cases, we have looked to the statute's 'legislative history' and 'surrounding circumstances' as well as to 'the face of the Act.'"). In the absence of an explicit statement on the face of the act, legislative history and circumstances can be used to show that Congress meant to abrogate Indian treaty rights.

The Court has developed a test to determine whether Congress intended to abrogate Indian treaty rights. In *Dion*, the Court held that for a treaty to be abrogated, there must be clear evidence that Congress actually considered the conflict between its intended action on the one hand and Indian treaty rights on the other, and it chose to resolve the conflict by abrogating the treaty. *Id.* at 739–40. The Court added that, while it would be "preferable" for Congress to explicitly state its intent to abrogate Indian treaty rights, it would be acceptable to present "sufficiently compelling" evidence in legislative history. *Id.* at 739. The result is that the *Dion* test must be met by sufficiently compelling evidence.

This is the most diffi-
cult part of this issue
for the petitioners —
the rest of this excerpt
is largely an attempt to
deal with negative au-
thority and to antici-
pate respondents' argu-
ments. Especially notice
how the brief avoids
saying things like "re-
spondents will argue."

In *Dion* itself the Court held that Congress abrogated Indian treaty rights with
the passage of the Bald Eagle Protection
Act. This result was based on the fact that
abrogation was "strongly suggested on the
face of the [act]" because it allows the taking of eagles for religious purposes by Indian tribes, and the legislative history of
the 1962 amendments which addressed Indian concerns about prohibiting the use of
eagle feathers. *Id.* at 740–41. Because the
Court decided that issue first, it did not decide whether the ESA also abrogated Indian treaty rights. The Court has never
held that the ESA abrogates Indian treaty-
reserved rights to hunt or fish.

In contrast to *Dion*, there is no evidence — much less sufficiently compelling
evidence — that Indian treaty rights were
considered in the ESA. There is nothing in
the legislative history of the ESA about Indian treaty rights. No evidence that Con-

gress actually considered the conflict between the ESA and Indian treaty rights. No evidence that it chose to abrogate Indian treaty rights. Thus, the ESA even fails the watered-down *Dion* test, and does not abrogate Indian treaty-reserved rights.

Again, note handling of negative authority.
Look back at this subsection and observe how the authors break the law into small increments and deal with each in turn.

The only court to find that the ESA abrogated Indian hunting rights reached that conclusion throught the misuse of the legislative histories of bills other than the ESA. H.R. 13081, 92nd Cong. 2nd Session; S. 3199, 92nd Cong., 2nd Session. 1972. In *United States v. Billie*, 667 F. Supp. 1485 (S.D. Fla. 1987), the court reviewed the histories of two other bills which were never enacted, but which had considered providing an exemption for Indian people to take species for religious purposes. *Id.* at 1490–91. These bills were never enacted because they did not express the will of Congress. It is inappropriate to use the legislative history of failed bills to interpret the ESA. The bill that did pass, the one at issue in this case, the ESA, is silent on the issue of Indian hunting, fishing and treaty rights.

In sum, there is no explicit statement of abrogation, and there is no legislative history of the ESA to suggest that Congress intended to abrogate Indian treaty rights. Therefore, there cannot be abrogation of treaty-reserved fishing rights. They are not contemplated in the ESA. The Confederated Tribes' treaty-reserved fishing rights are simply not within the scope of the ESA.

In this point heading, the brief focuses on the most dangerous part of the implicit abrogation argument for petitioners.

D.   **That The ESA Provides An Exemption For Alaska Native Subsistence Hunting Does Not Mean That Indian Treaty Rights Were Considered Then Abrogated.**

The exemption for Alaska Natives in the ESA has no relevance to Indian treaty rights. In *Billie*, the court decided that the ESA abrogates Indian treaty rights based on the fact that Congress chose to exempt certain Alaska Native subsistence activities. This conclusion is based on the flawed reasoning that because "other" Indians were not specifically exempted from the ESA they must be covered by it. The court decided "[we] infer that Congress must have known that the limited Alaskan exemption would be interpreted to show congressional intent not to exclude other Indians." *Id.* at 1491. That strained reasoning is simply not realistic. If the scope of a law were determined by what it did not say, Congress would have the impossible task of covering every eventuality when drafting a law. As a result, the *Billie* opinion "should not stand for the proposition that the inclusion of Alaskan natives' concerns in a statute is evidence that Congress has considered Indian treaty rights in the rest of the country." *United States v. Bressette*, 761 F. Supp. 658, 664 n2 (D. Minn. 1991).

The Confederated Tribes cannot be compared to Native Alaskans because the

Notice how the brief contains several different challenges to this line of reasoning, providing judges with multiple reasons to reject it.

latter do not have treaty rights. The U.S. government did not make treaties with Native Alaskans. So when drafting the exemption for Alaska Natives, Congress did not deal with the issue of treaty rights at all. Similarly, the *Billie* court was also not dealing with treaty-reserved rights because the Seminole reservations were established pursuant to an executive order that does not mention hunting and fishing rights. Although such rights may be implied as part of their larger rights of possession of the land, they were not explicitly provided for. The Confederated Tribes, on the other hand, have specific quantified treaty rights to fish. Thus the *Billie* decision does not apply here.

Other courts have also found that exemptions for Alaska Natives are not relevant to treaty rights analysis. For example, the Migratory Bird Treaty Act prohibits the sale of feathers from certain migratory birds and contains a similar exemption for "indigenous inhabitants of the State of Alaska to collect migratory birds for food and clothing." 16 U.S.C. §§ 704, 712. In *Bressette*, the court interpreted that exemption to be "irrelevant for purposes of treaty rights analysis because Alaskans do not have treaty rights." *Id.* at 663. In sum, exemptions for Alaska Natives in the ESA and other laws are not relevant to the analysis of Indian treaty rights.

Lastly, the Alaska Native exemption in the ESA should not be relevant to treaty-reserved rights because to treat them together assumes that Alaska Natives and Indians are the same peoples. It was plainly put in *Bressette* that "To treat the consideration of Native Alaskans' rights as the consideration of Native American treaty rights nationwide, for the simple reason that both groups are regarded as Indians, is disingenuous." *Id.* at 663. While the complexities of this issue are beyond the scope of this brief suffice it to say that this assumption is highly problematic and inappropriate to use as a basis for analysis.

It is therefore not relevant that the ESA provides an exemption for Alaska Natives. That exemption does not mean that all Indians' rights were considered and only Alaska Natives were selected to be exempt from the ESA. That exemption only means that Congress considered, then chose to exempt Alaska Natives. Indian treaty rights were not considered, and therefore not abrogated by the ESA. The Confederated Tribes' treaty-reserved fishing rights remain intact.

2. Excerpt from a Bad Brief

The following excerpt is an example of what not to do and is written on behalf of the respondents, the National Marine Fisheries Service and the U.S. Forest Service. This excerpt is not from an actual brief. Instead, it is an amalgamation of typical student mistakes.

We again suggest you start by reading the point headings. Note that, while they are phrased persuasively, they do not incorporate the legal standard, and they do not provide a synopsis of the steps in the argument. After reading just the headings, read the entire excerpt. Compare it to the excerpt above and see if you can determine where this brief goes wrong. Finally, read our annotations and see how they match the list of problems you discovered. Our annotations are not exhaustive, but rather just indicate the major problems.

ARGUMENT

The length of this heading is not bad, yet the sentence itself is wordy, making it difficult to follow.

I. THE ENDANGERED SPECIES ACT MANDATES THAT THE NATIONAL MARINE FISHERIES SERVICE AND THE FOREST SERVICE IMPOSE CONSERVATION MEASURES ON THE FISH AND ABROGATE THE CTCR'S TREATY-RESERVED FISHING RIGHTS TO ENSURE THE SURVIVAL OF THE SALMON

A. Respondents are subject to the Trust doctrine, which imposes upon the United States a duty to ensure the survival of the salmon for future generations of tribal members

It is poor form to have a quotation be a stand alone sentence — you should give it some context.

"Plenary authority over the tribal relations of the Indians has been exercised by Congress from the beginning, and the power has always been deemed a political one, not subject to be controlled by the judicial department of the government." *Lonewolf v. Hitchcock*, 187 U.S. 553 (1903). Since Congress is able to exercise this plenary power, Congress also holds a

The legal standard and the analysis have been intertwined here —

trust obligation to the CTCR which requires that it ensure the survival of the should lead with short clear statement of legal standard, and then proceed to analysis.

salmon in the Northwest. Congress has chosen to effectuate this obligation through the passage and enforcement of the Endangered Species Act (ESA). In addition to being a law that helps carry out the trust doctrine, the ESA is a law of general applicability, and Indians are United States citizens. That means they must follow the law, too. And the respondents' actions here were taken pursuant to their obligations under the ESA.

Note the failure to articulate the legal standard for treaty abrogation and the bare conclusory assertion. This is not persuasive.

Even if the ESA doesn't apply to the CTCR, Congress can abrogate a treaty whenever it wants to. That is a well-accepted principle of law and has been for a hundred years. *Lone Wolf v. Hitchcock*, 187 U.S. 553 (1903). Congress has chosen to abrogate the CTCR's treaty-based hunting and fishing rights with the enactment of the ESA.

The Plan created by the National Marine Fisheries Service was required under the ESA and mandates broad-sweeping conservation restrictions in order to preserve all the fish listed as Endangered. Even the Tribe agrees that conservation measures are necessary and will be effective in preventing the extinction of the salmon. Since the plan was required by the statute, and the statute is within Congress' power, and Congress can abrogate treaties, the respondents' plan abrogates the CTCR's treaty rights.

Poor sentence structure, making analysis and conclusion seem crammed in.

Heading contains mix and match legal standards.

B. <u>This Court has held that the government can impose conservation measures as long as the regulation is necessary for the conservation of the fish, thus allowing Congress to implicitly abrogate treaty hunting and fishing rights</u>

In addition to explicitly abrogating treaties, this Court has also said that Congress can implicitly abrogate a treaty, providing Congress' intention to do so is clear from the legislative history. *U.S. v. Dion*, 476 U.S. 734 (1986). The Court has developed a test to determine whether Congress

This subsection leads with a statement of the legal standard, but is not clear and easy to follow. Need to minimize use of complex/compound sentences.

intended to abrogate Indian treaty rights; the test says that Congress can abrogate Indian hunting and fishing rights in treaties provided the legislative history contains some indication that Congress knew there was a conflict between the Indian treaty-based hunting and fishing rights and the statute under consideration, that Congress thought about that conflict and chose to resolve that conflict by abrogating the Indian treaty-based hunting and fishing rights. *Dion*

Poor citation form.

This paragraph does not tie into legal standard in prior paragraph; it disrupts the flow of the argument.

NMFS Plan is necessary for the conservation of the fishes, because over a hundred years ago, salmon were so plentiful in the streams that it was said that one could walk across the rivers on the backs of the salmon. Now less than ten percent of those salmon remain. The NMFS Plan is designed to achieve the goal of preservation of the species as set forth by the federal mandates. The federal mandates require an increase in the numbers of each of the endangered species so those species can sustain themselves, and a conservation program to meet the needs of both Indians and non-Indians. After full consultation with all concerned parties, this general strategy was determined to best serve the interests of all affected parties.

The federal mandates require an increase in the numbers of each of the endangered species so those species can sustain themselves, and a conservation program to meet the needs of both Indians and non-Indians. After full consultation with all concerned parties, this general strategy was determined to best serve the interests of all affected parties.

The whole purpose of the ESA was to preserve species and their habitats. Congress decided when it passed that statute that conservation and preservation were paramount values, more important than the interests of any individual or any in-

Conclusory analysis—
need to explain each
step and not assume
the judges know what
you are thinking.

dustry. The evidence and legislative history shows that Congress knew that Indians possessed treaty hunting and fishing rights and that those rights might have to be abrogated. *United States v. Billie*, 667 F. Supp. 1485 (S.D. Fla. 1987). If a species is put on the endangered list, then the Indian treaty rights disappear, as tribes are subject to the rigors of the ESA just like everyone else.

Again, stand alone
quotations with no
context.

"The fishing rights do not persist down to the very last steelhead in the River." *Puyallup II.* "Rights can be controlled by the need to conserve a species;" and the time has come when the life of a species is so precarious that all fishing must be banned until the species regains assurance of survival." *Puyallup II.* "The Treaty does not give the Indians a federal right to pursue the last living steelhead until it enters their nets." *Puyallup II.*

Although conclusory
statements are gener-
ally okay in the conclu-

The NMFS has been ordered by the ESA to take conservation measures to ension paragraph, they need to be a logical step from an analysis that has already been explained. This brief never clearly laid out the law and the arguments. That means the judges would have to read it at least one more time to try and follow the arguments.

sure the survival of salmon. The NMFS authority emanates from Congress and is part of the fulfillment of federal obligations to Indians, including the trust responsibility. Because of the trust obligation, Congress must ensure the treaty right to fish in all usual and accustomed places. Only through the ESA will that treaty right be ensured for future generations.

Chapter 3

The Oral Argument

Now that you've finished (or at least made a good start) on your brief, you're ready to begin working on the oral argument. Make sure, however, to check the rules of your competition regarding faculty assistance and participation in practice rounds. Some competitions allow faculty or other coaches to conduct practice oral arguments from the moment the problem is released. Other competitions do not allow such practice rounds until the team has submitted its brief. You do not want to start your competition by violating the rules, so make sure you understand the boundaries.

This chapter is divided into two major sections: preparing the oral argument and scoring the oral argument. In the first section, we discuss how to go about structuring your oral argument and putting the various parts together. Most competition involve two preliminary rounds, and each team will argue for the petitioner/appellant in one round and the respondent/appellee in the other round. That means you will need to prepare for and practice both sides of the argument, not just the side you briefed. If your school is sending more than one team to the competition, the teams probably briefed different sides, and preparation for oral argument can begin by simply exchanging briefs and reading the arguments raised for the other side. Having more than one team also means that practices can be more realistic. If your school is sending only one team, however, do not feel that you are at a disadvantage. Just know that you will need to put a little more thought into your preparation and practice. In the "scoring" section, we discuss the general criteria used in most competitions to evaluate the performance of the participants.

A. Preparing the Oral Argument

Never forget that oral argument is an exercise in persuasion. It is, however, a specialized type of persuasion. This is not like a trial argument, where you basically give an emotional speech. In other words, this is *not* oratory. Oral argument is a conversation — a give and take between you and the judges. You should have a game plan and an idea of where you want to go and what you want the judges to do, but you do not have the same kind of absolute control that lawyers do in an opening statement or closing argument during an actual trial.

Consequently, preparation and flexibility are the key. This cannot be emphasized enough. The primary problem with ninety percent of oral arguments is a lack of preparation. While the judges do set the tone and ask the questions, you can have a good deal of influence on the substance of the oral argument, provided you are prepared with a strong introduction and have spent time anticipating possible questions and working out answers that properly focus the judges' attention.

Even though preparation and flexibility are key, the preparation involved must proceed along a specific path. Most students make the mistake of trying to put together their presentation by first writing out a speech. They then adapt the speech as needed based on whatever interruptions occur. This approach is detrimental, however, as it leads to insecurities and a lack of confidence in your argument, and, worst of all, a high likelihood of being surprised by the questions the judges might ask. So don't start by immediately scripting your remarks. Instead, you should begin your preparations by working on each of the separate pieces of the oral argument. Once you've created the pieces, you can then put the puzzle together.

In general, there are three sections to an oral argument: the introduction, the body, and the conclusion. This follows the standard format of public speaking: tell 'em what you're going to tell them, tell it to them, and then tell 'em what you told them. Again, though, do not fall into the trap of writing a speech. Rather, you need to first do the following things to start collecting your puzzle pieces:

1. Read the rules of the competition regarding time frame for argument, for rebuttal, and for rules about splitting arguments among the members of a team. Also check what the rules say you should do when you run out of time. One standard proce-

dure in oral argument is that if a judge asks you a question, and you run out of time to answer, you generally say something along the lines of, "Your Honor, I see my time is up. May I take a minute to answer your question?" Some competitions, however, flatly forbid this type of request. Make sure you know your competition's rules and use them during the practice sessions.

2. Check the competition rules to determine what court you are addressing — is it a federal court, a state court, or perhaps even an administrative court? Is it the first appellate court to rule, or has another appellate court already reviewed the case?

3. Know everything you can about the court, its jurisdictional reach, and how it works. How do cases get before the court? How much authority does the court have? What are the rules of the court?

Once you know the basics of the rules and procedures, it's time to start incorporating the substance of the competition problem. This is where your work on the brief will come in very handy. It never hurts, however, to double check your recollections of the underlying facts and rulings, as well as take a fresh look at some of the arguments. Make sure you can answer the following questions:

1. Know the record and the lower court opinion (if there is one) inside and out — what facts do you have? What implications can be made from those facts? How does all of that relate to each other?

2. What did the lower court(s) hold? Why? What reasons were given for each aspect of the decision?

3. Where do you think the lower court went wrong? Why? What should it have held? Why? (Remember, you will have to argue both sides of the case, so make sure you also build the argument in support of the lower court's decision.)

4. Know the law — know the opinions cited by the lower court inside and out. What are their citations? Their facts? Their holdings? How did the court use them? How should it have used them? Did the court misinterpret or misapply them? Should the court have used a different case altogether?

5. Double check your research — did you look at all the relevant journal articles, hornbooks, treatises, and reporters (including any specialized reporters)?

6. What are the various standards of review that apply to each issue? How do they affect your argument?

Once you can answer all these questions, you have most of the raw data you will need to build the oral argument. The following subsections will walk you through the process of converting that raw data into a polished oral argument. Before diving into the details, however, we want to alert you to two other preliminary steps.

First, if you haven't seen a competition style oral argument, you should see if you can find a videotape of one or two and watch them. We have opted not to reprint a transcript of an oral argument as part of this manual, as the flat words on the paper do not adequately convey the tempo, tone, and dynamics of an oral argument. Check with your coach and with your law library—are there videotape copies of prior oral argument rounds from your competition? From other appellate advocacy competitions? If there are no actual competition rounds, have any teams made videotapes of dress rehearsals? These can give you an overview of how an oral argument proceeds and what it looks like. If there are no videotapes of competition rounds, there might be a videotape of an appellate argument from a real case or a practitioner oriented video series that includes a mock oral argument. Be aware, however, that there are some differences between "real world" oral arguments and competition rounds. The biggest difference is that style tends to play a larger role in scoring competition rounds. Knowing the law and having the best legal argument is not enough—you must also master the presentation style.

You are now ready to decide what issues to raise at oral argument. These will generally track the issues raised in your brief, although you may have to winnow them down to the strongest two or three arguments. As you select your issues and walk through the process described below, you should also select a theme for your oral argument. This theme will help you phrase your issues during the introduction and decide how to answer the questions thrown at you by the judges. In addition to helping you with style and structure, the theme also helps you influence the judges' thought processes.

For example, let's draw upon the competition problem that provided the basis for the Brief excerpts set out in Chapter 2. Remember, that litigation involved the mythical Confederated Tribes of the Columbia River. A hundred years ago, the United States negotiated a treaty with the Confederated Tribes. In return for several million acres of land, the Confederated Tribes secured a promise that they could fish at all "usual and accustomed places" in perpetuity. Fish, and most particularly salmon, play a very large role in the social and religious life of the members of the Confederated Tribes. Under the facts of the problem, however, key species of fish were recently listed as Endangered, which triggered a duty by two federal agencies to create a plan to preserve those species of fish. As part of that plan, the federal agencies imposed a ten year moratorium on all fishing, including tribal fishing. The Confederated Tribes filed suit, alleging that the moratorium violated the Tribes' treaty fishing rights. The other issues in the competition revolved around whether the federal government failed in its trust responsibility toward the Tribes and whether the federal government improperly rejected the management plan proposed by the Tribes.

Given the facts, issues, and legal standards, the theme for the Tribes' oral argument could revolve around the fact that the federal government's arbitrary and capricious actions wiped out the Tribes' economy, culture, social structure, and religion for at least half a generation. Another possible theme could be that the federal government acted arbitrarily and capriciously when it restricted the actions of Indians, as all the scientific evidence indicated that the non-Indian businesses were the ones who had caused the decline of the fish population. Both themes were used successfully at the actual competition by different teams. The best theme for the attorneys representing the federal government was that the federal government had taken the minimum actions necessary to ensure that future generations of tribal members had access to the fish.

Thus, the theme should not be a bare statement of the law or a simple statement of facts. Rather, the theme should reinforce both your version of the law and your version of the facts. The theme should be a one sentence statement of the interpretive principle you want the court to use in constructing its opinion.

Now it's time to focus on the three stages of oral argument, each of which should be prepared separately: the introduction, the body, and the closing.

1. The Introduction

The introduction must accomplish a discrete set of purposes, and it must do so in no more than two minutes. Many (though not all) competition judges will let you set out your introduction without interruption. And indeed, this will probably be your only uninterrupted time, so you want to take advantage of it. On the other hand, the longer and more rambling your introduction, the more likely the judges are to jump in and start asking questions. So keep it succinct, but also take advantage of the fact that this is your chance to set the stage and the tone for the oral argument. The judges may or may not follow your lead, but you should at least give it a try.

Before going much further, we should explicitly address two preliminary, stylistic conventions. First, since most student competitions involve oral arguments presented to the U.S. Supreme Court, we will refer to the parties as petitioner and respondent. Remember, though, that one of the things you checked in the competition rules was the court to which you will be arguing. The proper terminology in your competition may be appellant/appellee or applicant/ respondent. Make sure you know the right term and use it. Second, the following discussion also assumes that each team consists of two students. Again, make sure you double check the rules of your competition and adapt the process accordingly. Some competitions allow three students on a team. This can be two oralists and a brief writer or all three can participate as oralists. If all three plan to take part in oral argument, make sure all three have practice time.

Both the petitioner and the respondent must fulfill certain requirements as part of their introduction. For the petitioner's side, however, the first student to speak has two extra responsibilities. Here's the checklist for each side, followed by a more detailed discussion of each stage:

<u>Team Member #1/Petitioner</u>

1. May it please the court
2. Introduce yourself & your partner
3. Tell who you represent
4. Reserve time for rebuttal
5. Roadmap of issues (signal who will address which issues)
6. Statement of facts
7. Transition

<u>Team Member #2/Petitioner</u>

1. May it please the court
2. Introduce yourself
3. Tell who you represent
4. Roadmap of issues
5. Transition

Team Member #1/Respondent

1. May it please the court
2. Introduce yourself & your partner
3. Tell who you represent
4. Roadmap of issues (signal who will address which issues)
5. Transition

Team Member #2/Respondent

1. May it please the court
2. Introduce yourself
3. Tell who you represent
4. Roadmap of your issues
5. Transition

Rebuttal (Team Member #1 or #2/Petitioner)

1. Roadmap of issue(s)
2. Transition

"**May it please the court.**" There are two schools of thought on where you should insert the phrase, "May it please the court." You *must*, however, use it in your first two sentences. The choice of where you place the phrase depends on your personal preference, your coach's preference, and where you are most likely to remember to use it.

The conventional wisdom says that "May it please the court" should be the first words out of your mouth when you walk up to the podium. So you would say, "May it please the court, my name is...." Then proceed to introduce yourself, your co-counsel, and continue with the rest of the introduction.

The second school of thought looks at the logic of the traditional opening sentence. Regardless of whether it pleases the court, your name is your name and your client is your client. Thus you would start by introducing yourself, your partner, and your client. *Then* say "may it please the court." If you are the first person to speak for the petitioner, you will next reserve time for rebuttal. The other three competitors will move directly into their roadmap.

Introduce yourself & your partner, and tell who you represent. This is just a one sentence identifier, "My name is [whatever], and along with my co-counsel [name], we are here today representing [client's name], the petitioner in this case." This structure also holds true for the first person who represents the respondent. If you are the second person up for either side, however, don't introduce your partner. Just introduce yourself and your client. There's no real need to reiterate whether your client is the petitioner or the respondent, just the client's name is usually sufficient.

Competitions where you present your argument to an international tribunal may require a slightly different form. Make sure you know what it is. For example, if you are arguing before the International Court of Justice, you will open with something like, "Madame/Mr. President, Your Excellencies, May it please the Court, My name is [whatever] and I am the agent for [Country Name]."

Always, always, always make sure you know the name of your client. It definitely starts things off on the wrong foot if you fumble your client's name or have to look it up. Once you've done the introduction, don't use the words "petitioner" or "respondent" again — it gets too hard for the court to remember who is who. Just use your client's name.

Reserve time for rebuttal. Check the competition rules about rebuttal. Even if the rules allow for rebuttal, only petitioners are entitled to it. So respondents will not say anything about rebuttal in their introduction. The first person to speak for petitioner, however, *must* explicitly reserve rebuttal time or you will forfeit it. The standard request is, "With the court's permission, we would like to reserve two minutes for rebuttal." Be prepared for the Chief Justice (the one sitting in the middle) to say "You may." The panel may, however, just nod. Remember, the rules of the competition may also require you to talk to the bailiff/timekeeper before the round to identify who will speak for how much time, including rebuttal.

Roadmap of issues. Once you've introduced yourself and your client (often called "putting your appearance on the record"), you will want to signpost briefly for the court the issues you are going to address in your argument. This serves as a road map for the judges, so they know what to expect. Also, if you get bogged down on your first issue for the entire time, then you at least were able to remind the judges of the other issues.

Two hints here. First, each member of the team should pick no more than two or three issues from the brief to discuss; these should be your best/strongest arguments. Your choice of how many issues may be driven by the problem. We have seen competition problems that contain more than ten issues, leaving the competitors many options as to which issues to focus on during oral argument. On the other hand, many competition problems contain only two to four issues, in which case you and your partner should divide them up in a way that results in the two of you addressing all the arguments. For example, if there are four issues in the problem, all of which are important, then you should take two and your partner should present the other two. The first person up for each side should signpost all the issues the team will cover and indicate which attorney will discuss which issue. In listing all the issues, the first competitor for each side should fully describe the issues she will be addressing, but can state her partner's issues in a more summary fashion, particularly if the issues are complex. The second team member for each side need only roadmap his issues. The idea is simply to signal to the judges what issues your team will cover in oral argument and who will cover each issue. Hopefully the judges will pick up on the division of responsibilities when they ask their questions; asking the appropriate questions of each competitor.

Second, state the issues in a persuasive fashion. There are two parts to a persuasive statement of the issues: the error and why it was wrong. You will want to keep your statement short and clear—something that can easily be followed aurally. Remember, the judges are listening to your spoken words, not reading a complex sentence on paper. Consequently, you generally want to state your issues in a positive, rather than a negative, fashion. In other words, don't depend on the word "not"—it is easy to miss when listening and then the judges are confused because they think you've just stated the opposite of what they expected. Sometimes you can't avoid the word "not," but make every effort to try. For example:

> The Kiowa Tribe asks this Court to reverse the Tenth Circuit and dismiss Hoover Industries' lawsuit, as Kiowa is a sovereign nation and has not waived its immunity.

> The Kiowa Tribe asks this Court to reverse the Tenth Circuit and dismiss Hoover Industries' lawsuit, as Kiowa is a sovereign nation and thus is immune from suit.

Statement of facts. The first competitor to speak for the petitioner should offer to provide the panel with a statement of the facts. This offer should be phrased something along the lines, "would your honors like a recitation of the facts?" Most of the time, the judges will decline because in competition they are more interested in how you handle the legal issues. You should be prepared, however, for the panel to say, "yes." Your statement of the facts should be an approximately sixty second version of the critical facts in the dispute. You want to provide the judges with enough background to understand the arguments you plan to present, but you don't want to get either them or yourself bogged down in every detail of the case. Don't forget you can cover some of the factual details during the body of your oral argument, as you flesh out your arguments.

The second person to speak for the petitioner should not offer a recitation of the facts. In addition, neither of the students representing the respondent are under any obligation to give a statement of facts. Occasionally, however, the resolution of the issues may revolve largely upon how the facts are characterized. In that event, the first student to speak for the respondent will want to deliver a statement of facts. If you do decide to give statement of facts, don't actually offer one — it will confuse the judges and make them think you don't know what you are doing. Instead, incorporate them as part of your transition. Give your roadmap, then say something like, "Your Honors, this case is not about [whatever the petitioners said]. Rather, it is about...." Then state your theme and proceed to deliver your version of the facts and transition to the body of the argument.

Transition. Finally, you will need to transition from the introduction into the body of your argument. This can be as simple as saying, "Turning to the first issue, [then briefly restate the first issue]." Sometimes, it may be more appropriate to use your theme as the transition. The choice depends on two things — your general preference and the complexity of the issues. The more complex the issues are, the more likely you are to want to use your theme, as it will help focus the judges and give them a handle on how to tie the issues together. If you use your theme, one typical approach would be to say, "Being treated equally does not always mean being treated the same. Here, the federal government has imposed restrictions on everyone unilaterally, regardless of fault. The government's approach is illegal, as illustrated by...." Then turn to a brief restatement of your first issue.

Putting all parts of the introduction together, it will look something like this:

Petitioner #1:

> May it please the Court, my name is Melissa Tatum and along with my co-counsel Barbara Bucholtz, we are here today representing the Confederated Tribes, the petitioners in this case. We would like to reserve two minutes for rebuttal. The Confederated Tribes ask this Court to reverse the Ninth Circuit. I will be addressing the first two issues. First, Congress did *not* abrogate the Tribes' treaty-guaranteed fishing rights when it passed the Endangered Species Act. Second, even if the government can regulate those rights, it must first impose all necessary restrictions on non-Indians before restricting treaty-guaranteed fishing. My co-counsel will address the other two issues, the government's duty to provide a moderate standard of living and the Tribes' right to co-manage the fisheries.

Would the Court like a recitation of the facts?

Being treated equally does not always mean being treated the same. Here, the federal government has imposed the same restrictions on all persons and industries, regardless of fault. The government's approach is illegal, however, as the Confederated Tribes are in a unique position: they hold treaty-guaranteed fishing rights. No other person or industry holds these rights. And the Tribes' rights were not abrogated by the Endangered Species Act because....

Petitioner #2:

May it please the Court, my name is Barbara Bucholtz and I represent the Confederated Tribes. This Court should reverse the Ninth Circuit, because the federal government's proposed plan is insufficient, as it fails to fulfill the government's treaty-based obligation to manage the fisheries in a way that will provide treaty fishermen with a moderate standard of living. In addition, the Tribes possess the right to co-manage the fisheries in order to protect their treaty-based rights. Turning to the first issue, the government's plan completely fails all of its obligations, as it does not manage the fisheries in a manner that will provide treaty fishermen with a moderate standard of living....

Respondent #1:

May it please the Court, my name is Martin Frey and along with my co-counsel Jane Begay, we are here today representing the National Marine Fisheries Service and the U.S. Forest Service, the respondents in this case. The federal government asks this Court to affirm the Ninth Circuit. I will be addressing the first two issues. First, the Tribes no longer possess treaty rights to fish, as Congress chose to abrogate those rights, deciding that they must give way to the exigencies of the Endangered Species Act. Second, this Court has repeatedly held that tribal fishing can be restricted when necessary to conserve species. My co-counsel will address the other two issues, that there is simply no governmental duty to provide a moderate standard of living nor are there any Tribal rights to co-manage the fisheries.

We agree that this is a case about fulfilling responsibilities. But the federal government has obligations not just to the current tribal fishermen, but to future generations of fishermen, as well as to the environment and the fish themselves. The Fisheries Service and the Forest Service have imposed the minimum restrictions necessary to fulfill all of these responsibilities. Turning to the first issue....

Respondent #2:

> May it please the Court, my name is Jane Begay and I represent the federal agencies involved in this suit. This Court should affirm the Ninth Circuit, as the federal government is under no obligation to provide Indian fishermen with a moderate standard of living. In addition, the ESA imposes upon the federal agencies a duty to manage the habitat as part of conserving the listed species. The Tribes do not share in that duty and have no right to co-manage the fisheries. Turning to the first issue....

Practice Tip: When conducting your practice rounds, you will certainly want to spend most of them doing complete run throughs of both sides, petitioner and respondent. You should also, however, spend one or two of your practice rounds just on the introduction, on the steps outlined above. Pay particular attention to the way you phrase your roadmap, the statement of the issues. You want it to be intelligible and convincing when spoken aloud. Remember, what reads well on paper does not always sound right when spoken, as spoken and written language can be very different. The more polished your introduction (and you should have it completely memorized—you shouldn't have to look down), the more likely the judges are to let you get through it uninterrupted.

2. The Body

As we stated earlier, you should not prepare for oral argument by writing out a speech. You should also avoid memorizing or even summarizing the written analysis in your brief. Written and oral discourse are two different "languages"—they have different strengths and require different strategies.

Rather, you should start your preparations by making an outline of your arguments. The major prongs of your outline are already written—they are the ones you created and delivered as the "roadmap" part of your introduction. Under each one of those major prongs, you want to create three subcategories of information: the relevant law, the critical facts, and how you want the court to apply the law to the facts. You may have several subcategories under each of these points (especially under the "how to apply the law to the facts" section), but keep them streamlined and simple. Always remember that after stating the issue itself, you should lead with your version of the legal standard. Many students dive directly into the facts of the case, and there is no quicker way to lose the judges or have them wander down a different path than you desire. Remember, you are arguing to an appellate court, which is concerned primarily with how to interpret the law and apply it to this case; the court is not, and cannot be, a fact-finder.

You should then do one or two practice sessions where you work with this outline, anticipating little or no questioning from the bench. This will allow you to streamline your arguments and cement them in your mind. Once you've got the basics of your argument, it's time to start adding in questions. And don't make the mistake of doing more than one or two practices without questions. Otherwise, you will get too set in your ways and will not be appropriately flexible in handling questions.

The best way to handle questions is to spend time anticipating what questions the panel is likely to ask and planning how you will respond. Competitions make this a bit easier, as you have to prepare both sides of the argument. That preparation should help you troubleshoot your case and identify the weak spots, whether they are factual problems or issues regarding the proper interpretation of the law. Be honest with yourself; don't sweep difficulties with your case under the rug, because you can bet the judges know about them and plan to grill you. The better job you do in identifying the difficult portions of your argument, the less likely you are to be surprised at oral argument; you will have already prepared answers to most of the questions the judges ask. You can never anticipate every question, but anticipation and preparation definitely show and will enhance your score. The judges are also more likely to cut you some slack if you don't have an answer to one or two curveballs, provided you've done well with the other questions. You are also likely to get downgraded if you haven't worked out solid answers to obvious questions.

The nature of moot court means that you must know the substance of the law, but that won't carry the day alone. In the real world, if you convince the judges that the law is on your side, they will rule in your client's favor. Most moot court judges are instructed to put aside the issue of who should win in the real world, and instead grade on performance during the round. Substance of the law is part of that performance, but so is presentation style. Unfortunately, the realities of moot court competition mean that style often becomes more important than substance. And nothing counts more in style than how you handle the panel's questions. A good answer has three parts:

1. **The Law.** Make sure you know the relevant legal principles and where they come from. Make sure that you have the case caption and citation ready in the event the judges ask for it. When you give your answer, you must tell the judges the relevant legal

principle. You do not, however, necessarily have to give the case caption, and you should not provide the actual citation unless asked. The decision whether to provide the case caption depends on two factors. First, how famous is the case itself? If it is very well known, especially if it is virtually synonymous with the legal principle (say, for example, *Miranda*), then by all means use the case name. Otherwise, it is easier to simply say "Tribal governments are sovereign entities, entitled to the sovereign's defense of immunity." The second factor is your personal preference and style. It is certainly acceptable to say, "As this court held in *Kiowa*, tribal governments are sovereign entities, entitled to the sovereign's defense of immunity."

2. **The Facts.** Make sure you know the facts of the problem inside and out, and make sure your answer incorporates the relevant facts. Make sure you also know where in the record those facts are located, in the event the court should ask. You do not, however, need to cite to the record unless requested to do so by a judge.

3. **The Transition.** After you answer the question, you must transition back into your argument. You want to return to your argument as gracefully as possible. The best oralists use the questions as tools — answer the question, but answer it in a way that you can use it to reinforce your arguments and your position, then work the answer to transition back into your argument. Don't leave a hanging pause or ask "does that answer your question?"; if the judge has a follow up question, the judge will interrupt again. Also, as part of your transition, you must decide where in your argument to return. One choice is to move back to where you were when the judge interrupted with a question. That will often be the best choice. The judge's question, however, may signal to you that the judges are most interested in your next point. In that case, it might be best to move ahead to that portion of your argument, and only after finishing it will you head back to finish up the argument you were making when interrupted.

There are a number of standard conventions you should be aware of in handling questions from the bench. First and foremost, however, do not act resentful of the questions. Questions are the heart and soul of oral argument. They are the primary factor the judges will use in evaluating your performance at oral argument. You should also welcome questions because they signal that the judge is listening and paying attention. Thus, you should always, always allow the judge to interrupt you with a question, no matter what you are saying. If the judge opens his or her mouth, you shut yours automatically — only one person should talk at a time, and judges get priority. It doesn't matter how important the point is that you are making or that you have only four more words and you're done. The judge starts to talk, and you stop. Immediately. Also, make sure you respond to the question asked. This has three components:

1. Answer immediately. Never say, "I'll get to that shortly," even if the question totally disrupts your organization. Worse yet, never say, "That is addressed in my brief." And try not to say "my partner will answer that." The judge does not want to wait. It would be acceptable to provide a very brief answer and then indicate that co-counsel will address the issue more fully. If the judge pushes the issue, however, you need to be prepared with a more detailed response.

2. If the question calls for a yes or no answer, begin your response with "Yes, your honor" or "No, your honor," and only then go on to explain.

3. Answer the question asked. Listen carefully to the exact question, and respond to it, not to the question you would have like the court to ask. Do not say, "I think you are really asking...."

Other conventions of answering questions include:

1. Always address the judge as "your honor." In most competitions, since you are arguing to the Supreme Court, the panel consists of "justices," not "judges." You can refer to them as "judge" or "Ms. Justice," but it is safer to get into the habit of using the always appropriate "your honor."

2. Remember to stay professional at all times. While you are technically competing for your own sake, the format of the competition is structured so that you are an attorney representing a client. You must put your client's interests first. So keep your response targeted at answering the question, not responding to the judge's tone. In other words, don't get irritated, flustered, or argumentative. You are always free to disagree with a judge, but do so in a civil manner.

3. Don't signal to the judge, either verbally or with body language, that you think the question is irrelevant or stupid. The judge

asked the question, so the judge wants an answer and thinks that answer is important.

4. If you do not understand a judge's question, it is perfectly acceptable to ask the judge to ask for clarification. You can ask the judge to repeat the question, rephrase the question, or you can indicate that you are not sure you understood the question and then you can rephrase it and ask if your understanding is correct. But don't ask more than once. If you've already asked the judge to repeat the question, but you still do not understand it, try your best to answer it. If the judge doesn't think you answered, the judge will ask the question again.

5. Finally, don't try to evade a question, either because you don't know the answer or because it exposes a major weakness in your case. The judges will be watching for this, and you can bet they will know what you are doing. If you don't know the answer, say so. If the question exposes a major weakness in your case, you have hopefully already anticipated the question and worked out an answer. If you haven't, then just give it your best shot.

There are an infinite number of questions judges may ask; the possibilities are almost limitless. There are, however, some standard categories of questions. Approximately seventy percent of the questions you are likely to hear fall in these standard categories:

1. Explain some of the background facts of the case at bar.

2. Clarify the facts, holding or reasoning of a case you cite.

3. Explain why a case supports your position, or why contrary authority should not control the court's decision.

4. Explain the ramifications of applying the principles you advocate.

5. Explain how deciding the case in your client's interest would impact public policy.

6. Explain why the result you want would be fair or equitable.

Remember, fundamentally, the judges control oral argument with their ability to ask questions. You exercise some control through signposting and working the answers to the questions, but if the judges want to take you somewhere, let them. If it's a tangent, answer it concisely and then work back into the important stuff. This is where the importance of brainstorming, practice, anticipation, and preparation comes into play. Work with people who know the problem, who know only the general area, and who know nothing about the area at all. They will help you anticipate a variety of angles and how to work them.

Before wrapping up this section, we should say a final word about hot and cold courts. You will hear these terms used in two different ways: preparation of the panel and questioning by the panel. In terms of preparation, a "hot court" is one who has read the bench brief and is prepared and knowledgeable about the case. Most moot court judges will fall into this category, as they understand its importance in terms of properly evaluating the participants. A "cold court," conversely, is one that is not prepared. While you are not likely to get a completely unprepared panel in a competition (although it is possible), you are likely to see a variety of levels of knowledge about the problem itself, as well as about the background of this particular area of law. This is when your preparation comes into play. By practicing in front of judges with varying levels of understanding and knowledge, you will be better able to anticipate the types of questions you will be asked.

In terms of questioning, a "hot court" is one that asks a lot of questions. A "cold court" would be one that asks very few questions. There is no way to tell what kind of court you will have before you walk into the room. That's why you need to practice before both types of panels. You will want to have enough information prepared to fill your time, even with minimal questions, but you don't want to get so locked into a particular rhythm or content that you get flustered when you are interrupted with questions. If you do have a cold court, however, it is quite likely that you will not use all your time. There is nothing wrong with wrapping up two or three minutes early if the panel is not actively asking you questions.

3. The Closing

Finally, you will also need to prepare two versions of your closing — the "ten seconds and I'm out of time" version and the "I have a minute or two to wrap up" version. Watch your time and honor the clock — always leave yourself at least ten seconds to close. Sometimes the judges will keep you talking past the stop signal or the end of your allotted time. If this happens, say something courteous like, "Your Honor, I see my time is up, may I finish answering your question?" (provided, of course, the rules of the competition allow you to do so). The judge will almost always say yes. Do a quick answer to the question, and then squeeze in your ten second closer.

The short closer is literally just one sentence, the action you want the court to take and a conclusory statement of why. For example, "Your Honors, the Government asks that you uphold the decision of the lower court, as it committed no reversible errors."

The longer conclusion will in many ways mirror your opening statement. Begin by stating the action your client wants the court to take — "Your Honors, the Cherokee Nation asks that you reverse the court of appeals, ..." Then give the reasons why the court should take that action. These reasons will mirror the issues listed in the roadmap portion of your introduction.

Regardless of which version of the conclusion you use, make sure to say "Thank you" at the end, and then sit down.

4. Putting It All Together

During your practices and at the competition itself, you will need to put all these pieces together. We tell you how to do that in this section, by walking you through what happens in the competition room, what to take to the podium, and a final reminder of the major stylistic conventions governing oral argument.

a. What Happens in the Competition Room

Most moot courts have a panel of judges, headed by a chief judge who orchestrates the proceedings. There is also, generally, a bailiff or time-keeper who helps you keep track of your allotted time. If at all possible, you should arrive at your assigned room at least five or ten minutes early. If you have enough advance notice of what room you are competing in, then go check it out, see how the room is laid out, and get a feel for it. Once you arrive at the room before your round, you should probably check in with the bailiff, if there is one. The bailiff will need to know you are present and may also need to ask questions about how the team is dividing its allotted time.

The bailiff will also generally open the court session. Make sure you stand when the bailiff begins the "hear ye, hear ye" (or "oyez, oyez") speech. Don't sit until instructed to do so by the judges. They will generally say "you may be seated," but they may also just waive you to your seats. Be alert. You should also watch the panel as they get settled. The judges will need to organize their paperwork, get the score sheets and notepads arranged, and may need to ask you for information, such as your names and team number, to finish filling out their score sheets. The panel may also ask both sides if they are ready. The judges will then either look at you expectantly, or one of them may explicitly state "petitioners, you may proceed." In either case, the first speaker for the petitioners should approach the podium, make eye contact with all the judges to ensure they are ready and paying attention, and then should begin the oral argument. Deliver it as developed above: moving from the introduction into the body and then into the conclusion. Once you've run out of time or have delivered your conclusion, say "thank you" and sit down.

Each subsequent speaker should automatically go to the podium when the prior speaker finishes. But don't begin your presentation until all the judges have made eye contact or until one of the judges tells you to proceed. The panel will need a few moments to make notes. The presentations proceed in the following order:

- Petitioner #1
- Petitioner #2
- Respondent #1
- Respondent #2
- Rebuttal (Petitioner #1 or #2)

In addition to following the introduction, body, closing game plan outlined above, respondents will want to do one additional thing: notice what questions the court asks the petitioners. If the Court's discussion seems to favor your argument, make a note of the judge's rationale and use it in your argument. Additionally, you may also want to refute directly some argument made by your opponent.

The rebuttal will be delivered by one (but only one) of the team members representing the petitioners. Some competitions may require you to identify in advance who will deliver the rebuttal. Other competitions are more flexible. In the flexible competitions, you and your partner will need to make a choice—is one of you a better speaker or more comfortable giving the rebuttal? If so, that's the person who should plan on delivering the rebuttal, and you should practice that way. If both of you are equally comfortable at the podium and adept at a rebuttal style presentation, then you may want to see what your opponents argue and the focus of the panel's questions. The team member more knowledgeable about that issue should be the one to approach the podium and deliver the rebuttal.

The rebuttal is a specialized type of oral argument. Remember, if you want to reserve the possibility of rebuttal, the first speaker for the petitioner must explicitly reserve the time. Check the rules of your competition to see how much time you can allot for rebuttal. In any event, however, you will generally want to reserve one of three quantities: one minute, a minute and a half, or two minutes. Any less than one minute, and you won't have enough time to say anything meaningful. Any more than two minutes, and you will unduly diminish the time for the bulk of your main argument, as well as give the judges too much time to ask more questions.

Just because you reserve time for rebuttal, however, doesn't mean that you must deliver one. Whether to give a rebuttal, and what you should say in one, depends upon the panel's questions to both sides and the points made by the respondents. It is perfectly acceptable for one of the team members to approach the podium after respondents have finished and say something like, "your honors, the petitioners waive rebuttal." The judges generally will say okay and let you sit down. Be prepared, however, for them to say, "counselor, just one more question...." You will then have to answer it.

We generally advise our students not to waive rebuttal, even if it is allowed. Rebuttal is your chance as petitioner to have the final say, and to leave the panel with your words ringing in their ears. To be effective, however, you should plan to make no more than one or two points in your rebuttal. What these points are will usually vary, depending on the focus of the respondents and the judges. You may want to correct a statement of fact, point the judges to another case, or something else along these lines. If you don't feel anything needs to be corrected, then just give a slightly abbreviated version of your and your partner's roadmaps — remind the court how you want it to rule and why.

In some competitions, once the round is concluded, the judges will give you feedback and critiques immediately. In these competitions, the bailiff will generally take you outside the room to wait while the judges conference and fill out their ballots. Then the bailiff will bring you back in the room for a five to ten minute critique.

b. What To Bring to the Podium

Now that you understand how an oral argument works and what happens in the competition round itself, we need to say a few words about what material you should bring to the round and what you should take with you to the podium. When you approach the podium to speak, the only thing you should have in your hands is a letter sized manila file folder. You will actually have two file folders: one for petitioner and one for respondent.

When you reach the podium, open the folder and place it on the podium. (Make sure you've take the right one — you don't want to start delivering the other side's argument for them!) The left side of the folder should contain two things. At the top should be a clearly printed reminder of your client's name and what side you are representing, petitioner or respondent. The other item is an $8\frac{1}{2} \times 11$ inch sheet of paper, which should be firmly stapled in place. That page will contain all three parts of your argument: the introduction, the outline version of the body of the argument, and the two versions of the conclusion. You should use a large enough typeface to be easily readable at a glance. By keeping the information to the bare bones, you also insure that you do not become overly reliant on a written speech. Remember, you want to keep your presentation as conversational as possible.

The right side of the folder should be used for listing the case caption, citation, and important holdings of all the key cases. You can do this by putting it all on one $8\frac{1}{2} \times 11$ sheet of paper and stapling it in, or you can use notecards. If you use notecards, they should be arranged in a waterfall or cascade, with the top of each card firmly affixed. You can then flip through the cards with no fear that they will come loose. Indeed, you do not want to be shuffling paper or cards of any kind during your talk. They make noise and can be dropped, creating an embarrassing distraction. That's the entire reason behind the manila folder approach.

You should also have in the room with you a complete copy of the record, as well as complete copies of all key cases and law review articles. That way you can quickly reference the text if needed. These items are best organized in tabbed, three ring binders and put within easy reach on the counsel table. An alert partner can help you find things quickly in the event the judges press you on something you don't have at the podium.

c. A Final Checklist of Oral Argument Stylistic Conventions

When delivering your oral argument, remember that this is a conversation, but you are a professional, representing a client. To be an effective advocate you need to be cognizant of your body language and intonation. All the standard items taught in any public speaking course. We've included a list of the major topics below. Also remember, however, that while you should always be deferential, courteous and responsive to the Court, you should not hesitate to maintain your position on the issues. If you don't know something, don't be afraid to acknowledge it. Be flexible after addressing a question posed by the court and try to think of a way to use that dialogue to segue back to your argument. Use the question posed to reiterate your line of reasoning and logic.

In addition:

1. Be yourself. Remember, this is a dialogue, not a theatrical performance. You should not try to present a different persona or use a style with which you are not comfortable. The best style is one that is confident, but not arrogant; respectful, but not obsequious.

2. Don't just read a speech or recite memorized words — engage the judges in a persuasive dialogue designed to demonstrate that you have the best interpretation of the law and the best argument for how that law should be applied to the facts.

3. While at the podium, keep your feet approximately shoulder width apart and keep your weight evenly distributed on both feet. Don't slump. And whatever you do, don't walk around, shuffle your feet, or sway. It's distracting, and you want to keep the judges focused on the content of your argument.

4. Watch your body language. Don't fiddle with pens, notecards, paperclips or rings. Again, it's distracting. If you are comfortable making gestures, you may make a few, provided you keep them natural, small, and minimal. Grand gestures or lots of hand wavy stuff is distracting. It's best to keep your hands at your side or resting lightly on the podium. (Don't use a white-knuckled death grip on the sides of the podium!)

5. Watch your intonation. Keep your voice well modulated and speak at a comfortable listening speed. Too slow, and the judges will jump in with questions. Too fast, and they can't understand what you are saying. You should always speak clearly and distinctly.

6. Make and maintain eye contact with the judges. Show them that you know your position and are confident of it. Eye contact helps maintain the conversational style.

7. Don't be intimidated by the atmosphere or the questions. This is where preparation becomes key — the more you practice, the more time you spend anticipating questions and planning answers, the better job you will do at avoiding the intimidation factor.

8. Avoid making personal attacks either on the panel or on opposing counsel. Remember, you will get further by convincing the panel you have the best argument, not by belittling the lower court or the opposing side.

9. While at the counsel table, pass notes with your co-counsel only when necessary. Avoid whispering and making faces while your opponents are speaking.

B. Scoring the Oral Argument

This chapter would not be complete without saying a word about the judges and the scoring criteria. You are likely to see a wide variety of judges, although all of them are likely to be lawyers. Some may be recent graduates, some may be experienced attorneys, some may be law professors, and some may even be judges in real life. Some will have a wealth of knowledge about this area of the law, and some may know only what was in the bench brief. This mean you will hear a variety of different questions and be critiqued on a variety of different matters. You are also likely to hear conflicting advice. You will just have to do your best to balance the conflicting input with your own judgment and experience, as well as with your coach's teachings.

The judging ballots will also vary among the competitions. Some ask a number of detailed questions and ask the judge to score each competitor in each category, and then total up the numbers. Some contain just a brief list of five or six factors the judges should consider and then simply ask the judge to assign each competitor one numerical score. Competition ballots will also vary in their emphasis: do they focus the judges' attention primarily on the competitor's substantive knowledge, their presentation style, or does the ballot balance the two equally? Although the emphasis will vary, there is a relatively standard list of factors judges will consider in evaluating each competitor:

1. **General Courtroom Manner.** This covers general matters of poise, appearance (are you in proper court attire?), courtroom decorum, and respect for the court.

2. **Answering Questions.** How well did you answer the court's questions? Were your questions responsive and accurate? Did you use the questions to your advantage?

3. **Returning to Argument.** How well did you transition from your answer back into your argument? Was your presentation flexible?

4. **Clarity of Presentation.** How well did you present the points of your argument? Were they clear and logical? Did you mislead the court about any of the law or facts?

5. **Familiarity with the Law.** Did you know the relevant legal principles? Were you familiar with the key cases?

6. **Familiarity with the Record.** Did you know the relevant facts? Could you find things in the record if asked? Did you know the procedural history of the case?

7. **Speaking Ability and Delivery.** Did you have a good presentation style? Did you make eye contact? How was your body language? Intonation and inflection? Did you move around or fiddle with pens? How persuasive were you?

Finally, some ballots will contain a catch all category, called something along the lines of "overall performance." This category will allow the judge to pull all the diverse factors together and score the overall impact of your performance.

You are now ready to compete successfully in any appellate advocacy competition. Our only remaining piece of advice is that you keep in mind that "success" is not limited to bringing home a trophy. The entire competition and preparation process is a tremendous learning experience. You should evaluate your success based on what you learned and how you improved, not on whether you win a trophy.

Good Luck!

Part II

Non-Brief Writing Competitions

The early 1970s and 1980s saw judges, law professors, and attorneys give greater emphasis to methods of dispute resolution other than litigation. The grouping of non-litigation methods became known as the ADR movement. Today, each federal district court is required to offer litigants some form of ADR, some state courts also provide litigants a forum for ADR, the American Bar Association has created a Section of Dispute Resolution, many law school offer ADR courses (*e.g.*, Introduction to ADR; Interviewing, Counseling and Negotiating; Mediation; and Arbitration), several law schools offer ADR certificates as part of their JD program, several offer Master of Laws degrees in ADR, and some even have student staffed ADR journals. The legal climate is changing, leading attorneys to accept ADR as a part of their practice and some judges express the belief that attorneys commit malpractice when they fail to advise their clients about the availability of ADR.

In light of this changing environment, the American Bar Association's Law Student Division now sponsors the ABA/LSD Negotiation Competition and the ABA/LSD Client Counseling Competition and the ABA's Section of Dispute Resolution sponsors the ABA Mediation Advocacy Competition. Unlike the Appellate Advocacy Competitions, these competitions do not require a written brief. They require a different set of skills and it is these skills that will be addressed in the next three chapters.

Chapter 4

Interviewing and Counseling Your Client

This chapter on interviewing and counseling demonstrates how to develop skills for the Client Counseling Competition. In practice, attorneys will first interview potential clients to learn about their problems and to decide whether to offer to represent them. A number of factors may lead to a decision not to represent a potential client. The person being interviewed may have a problem that is not within the attorney's realm of expertise, or the attorney may discover a conflict of interest, or the attorney may not want that person as a client. Or the person being interviewed may not want to hire the attorney. If the person being interviewed does become the attorney's client, the attorney must then counsel the client as to the problem and the processes available for resolving the problem. Depending on the complexity of the client's problem and the urgency with which action must be taken, the counseling session maybe held several days or weeks after the initial interview. (For the sake of simplicity, we will refer to the person being interviewed as the client rather than the potential client. The student-attorneys will be referred to as the attorneys or the team.)

To some extent, the ABA/LSD Client Counseling Competition replicates the real world of practice. Under the ABA/LSD *Client Counseling Competition Rules and Standards for Judging*, each team (two students per team) will be provided confidential facts for three problems (*i.e.,* "the consultation situations") no sooner than ten days prior to the date of the competition. This information will be similar to that solicited from the client by the attorney's secretary when the client calls for an appointment. Examples of prior years' consultation situations (*Explanation and Consultation Situations*) are available for a fee from the Law Student Division of the ABA. *See* ABA/LSD *Client Counseling Competition Rules and Standards for Judging*, art. X.

During the competition, each team will have thirty minutes to interview and counsel the client. This is referred to in the *Rules and Standards for Judging* as the "consultation." The consultation is followed by a fifteen minute "post-consultation." The client, who has received confidential facts, will participate in the consultation but will not participate in the post-consultation. During the post-consultation the attorneys have an opportunity to demonstrate to the judges:

> [that they have] recognized their own and the client's feelings, the strengths and limitations of their interviewing and counseling skills, their handling of the substantive aspects of the client's problems (legal and non-legal), and provided for an effective follow-up.

ABA/LSD *Client Counseling Competition Standards for Judging*, standard 10.

Therefore, during the post-consultation the attorneys may critique the consultation, dictate memorandum, and discuss the legal issues to be researched and other legal work to be done. Both the consultation and the post-consultation will take place before the judges. No subsequent counseling session will take place.

A team may use books, notes, charts, and office props (dictation equipment, files, and desktop furnishings) during the consultation and the post-consultation. The judges, however, are advised not to give undue weight to these materials or props.

Generally, a Client Counseling Competition will involve four rounds. All teams compete in the first three rounds. These rounds are conducted simultaneously so a team could compete in round three (Problem 3) before competing in round one (Problem 1). A three judge panel is assigned three teams. After observing all three teams, each judge will rank each team one, two, or three with one being the best score. After all teams have completed three rounds, the three teams with the lowest scores will advance to the fourth and final round.

Under the ABA/LSD *Client Counseling Competition Rules and Standards for Judging*, a team may work closely with its coach on all aspects of the competition "up to the moment when the actual performance begins." *See Rules and Standards for Judging*, art. XIV.

A. The Consultation

The consultation includes the kinds of discussions that transpire in a client interview in practice. In addition, the consultation in competitions includes aspect of what could be in a separate counseling session. The thirty minute consultation can be structured into five segments — getting acquainted, gathering facts and feelings, establishing the attorney/client relationship, proposing a solution or a process for resolving the problem, and wrapping up.

But before the consultation can begin, you must prepare. Preparation is the key to a good consultation. Because you will need to cover substantial ground during the thirty minute consultation, carefully plan how long you will devote to each of the five segments of the consultation. For example:

3 minutes	getting acquainted
15 minutes	gathering facts and feelings
5 minutes	establishing the attorney/client relationship
5 minutes	proposing a solution or a process for resolving the problem
<u>2 minutes</u>	wrapping up
30 minutes	

1. Preparing for the Consultation

Consider doing the following before the consultation:

1. Carefully review the rules for the competition. Know how the competition will be organized. Know what you can and cannot do. Know the criteria upon which you will be judged.

2. Learn something about the client (*i.e.*, the person in the problem). Begin with the consultation situation that you received from your secretary (*i.e.*, the confidential facts). All teams will receive the same confidential facts. Be creative and expand upon these facts. If the client is a public figure, public information is available. For example, check the print media and the internet. If the client is a professional, learn something about the client's profession. If the client buys or sells a commodity, learn something about that commodity and the industry that deals in that commodity. If the client has been involved in an incident or event, learn something about that incident or event.

3. Organize what your client has told your secretary (the consulta-
    tion situation) in chronological order. Think about what facts
    are missing from this chronology. Prepare a written time line
    (chronology) for use during the consultation. Know the order of
    events.

4. Learn something about your client's perception of the problem.
    Again, carefully review the consultation situation. Also read be-
    tween the lines to understand your client's feelings. Most prob-
    lems have both a fact and a feelings component. Why does your
    client seek this consultation? What do you perceive to be your
    client's goals?

5. Once you feel you know your client's perception of the prob-
    lem, you can prepare for the substance of the consultation. For
    example, a basic understanding of the elements of a potential
    cause of action would be helpful once you have had the oppor-
    tunity to help your client fully develop your client's version of
    the story.

6. Begin a conflict of interest check. Is there any reason why you
    cannot represent this person, partnership, or corporation?

7. Prepare drafts of documents that you may use during the con-
    sultation, including the attorney/client contract which includes
    a discussion of fees. Sample contracts can be found on the inter-
    net and in form books. Prior to the competition, all teams will
    be provided a uniform fee schedule. You must use the uniform
    fee schedule.

8. Prepare your personal appearance and the appearance of the
    consultation room. How do you want to be perceived? First im-
    pressions are extremely important. Turn off your mobile phone,
    your pager, and the alarm on your watch.

9. Prepare to begin the consultation on time and to end the consul-
    tation within the allotted time of thirty minutes. You must keep
    your own time and if you exceed the thirty minutes, it will
    shorten the time for your post-consultation. Both the consulta-
    tion and the post-consultation will be observed, evaluated, and
    scored by the judges.

    Since two students are on a team and both are serving as attor-
    neys, both must actively participate in the consultation. Participa-
    tion must be balanced. Decide before the competition how you
    will work together as a team. Who will be responsible for which

part of the consultation? Who will watch the time so all aspects of the consultation are covered during the thirty minutes?

2. Conducting the Consultation

As previously noted, the thirty minute consultation can be structured in five segments—getting acquainted, gathering facts and feelings, establishing the attorney/client relationship, proposing a solution or a process for resolving the problem, and wrapping up.

a. Getting Acquainted

Beginning the consultation can be awkward, especially if the consultation is your first meeting with your client. You, as the attorney, need to put your client at ease and establish that you are in charge. Begin the consultation by:

1. Greeting your client in the reception area (Include a firm handshake, if appropriate)

2. Escorting your client to the consultation room

3. Introducing your client to your co-counsel

4. Showing your client where to sit

Rather than abruptly plunging into the subject of "why are you here?" consider beginning with a few minutes of non-threatening conversation. Learn about your client as a person. Most people enjoy talking about themselves. Information gathered in preparing for the consultation may provide you with discussion topics. After spending a few minutes, you will get a sense that your client is ready to tell you about what brought him or her to you.

b. Gathering Facts and Feelings

Gathering facts and feelings, the heart of the consultation, has three distinct phases—listening, developing, and confirming.

i. Listen to Your Client's Story

The first phase of gathering facts and feelings, listening, is totally client centered. You, as the attorney, begin this listening phase by giving your client instructions as to where to begin the story, where to end the story, and how much detail to reveal during the telling of the story. Once you have given these instructions, your client will do all the speaking and you should listen and not interrupt. By listening without interrupting, you provide your client the opportunity to tell the story in the client's own words, including what the client believes is important and omitting what the client believes is less important.

You must listen very carefully. Not everything clients tell their attorneys is important, although they may have a great need to do so. Also not everything clients do not tell their attorney is unimportant. Clients may be motivated to hide or distort the facts. They may believe that by telling certain facts they will jeopardize their case or place themselves in a poor light and therefore they withhold these facts. Some clients may be uncomfortable to relate personal details to a stranger or to relive traumatic events. Some clients embellish upon the facts, some distort the facts, and some even lie.

Do not interrupt your client even though there is something you really must know. Make a note of what you want to know and you will have your opportunity to ask in the next phase of the fact and feeling gathering segment.

The listening phase could be diagramed to look like this:

attorney's one open ended question ————————————————>
<........................ client's
<........................ multiple
<........................ statements
<........................ in response
<........................ (*i.e.*, client's
<........................ story)

As you listen, check the time line that you prepared prior to the consultation. Note where gaps in information occur.

ii. Develop Your Client's Story

The second phase of gathering facts and feelings gives you, as the attorney, the opportunity to expand and focus your client's story. During this phase, your client's story is developed fully, from beginning to end. Also, you have the opportunity to develop fully those facts relevant to your client's legal position. During the listening phase, your client may have had a greater need to develop facts other than those essential to your client's legal position. Your client also may have had personal reasons for not presenting all these facts to you. The story development phase gives you the opportunity to fully explore what has consciously or subconsciously been omitted from the client's narrative.

During the story development phase, you have the opportunity to develop your client's story your way. Do not conclude this phase of the interview until you know all that you want to know.

As you progress though the story development phase, be specific in seeking out information. Your client may have brought documents including insurance policies, letters, e-mails, reports, canceled checks, written offers and contracts, written warranties, subpoenas, and transcriptions of depositions. Your client may be able to provide you with lists of witnesses and other interested parties including their names, addresses, telephone numbers, and relationship to the problem, and your client may also have other information such as photographs, diagrams, and tape recordings. Ask for them.

The story development phase, when diagramed, would look like this:

First Topic on the Time Line

attorney's open ended question   ——————————————————->
                                 <.....................client's multiple
                                 <.....................statements in
                                 <.....................response

attorney's follow-up open ended question   ——————————————->
                                 <.....................client's
                                 <.....................response

attorney's narrow follow-up question   ————————————————->
                                 <.....................client's response

attorney's narrow follow-up question   ————————————————->
                                 <.....................client's response

attorney's narrow follow-up question   ————————————————->
                                 <.....................client's response

Second Topic on the Time Line

attorney's open ended question   ——————————————————->
                                 <.....................client's multiple
                                 <.....................statements in
                                 <.....................response

attorney's follow-up open ended question   ——————————————->
                                 <.....................client's
                                 <.....................response

attorney's narrow follow-up question   ————————————>
<...................client's response

attorney's narrow follow-up question   ————————————>
<...................client's response

attorney's narrow follow-up question   ————————————>
<...................client's response

Third Topic on the Time Line

....

Fourth Topic on the Time Line

....

Continue until all topics on the time line have been explored.

End the story development phase by asking how your client would like the problem resolved. Again, ask an open ended question and then explore and expand your client's response with a series of narrow questions.

iii. Confirm What You Perceive To Be Your Client's Story

The third phase of gathering facts and feelings segment provides you an opportunity to confirm your perceptions of your client's story. This phase also gives your client an opportunity to correct your misperceptions or to add information that either was not previously conveyed to you or was overlooked by you.

A diagram of this third phase, the story confirmation phase, would look like this:

The Attorney Would Review the Facts in Chronological Order Ending with How the Client Would Like the Problem Resolved

attorney's leading question or statement   ———————————>
<.........................client's affirmation

attorney's leading question or statement   ———————————>
<...................client's correction of misperception

attorney's leading question or statement   ———————————>
<.........................client's affirmation

attorney's leading question or statement   ———————————>
<........................client's partial affirmation
<........................and clarification

Continue until all relevant facts have been confirmed. Also confirm how the client wants the problem resolved.

c. Establishing the Attorney/Client Relationship

The third segment of the consultation, establishing the attorney/client relationship, is the business segment of the consultation. During this segment the person being interviewed either becomes or does not become your client.

i. Commit to the Person Being Interviewed and that Person's Case

Not every person you interview will become your client. After hearing the story, you may decide not to take the case for a variety of reasons. The prospective client may reveal facts that create a conflict of interest for you, or place the problem beyond the scope of your practice, or require you to do something that is unethical or illegal. Or the problem may involve more time than you have to devote to the matter.

If, for some reason you decide you cannot represent this person, then it is at this point in the consultation that you say "Sorry but...." You may, if you believe it appropriate, provide the person interviewed with a list of attorneys who might be interested in providing representation.

ii. Discuss the Attorney/Client Contract

If you agree to represent the prospective client, the focus shifts from you to the client. Does that person want your representation? Before an educated determination can be made, the client must know what your representation will include and what your representation will cost.

At this point it is not only appropriate but imperative for you to review the written contract for services. Note that prior to the consultation you had prepared drafts of attorney/client contracts. Depending on the information you received from your secretary who made the appointment, it may be appropriate to prepare several contract forms (e.g., fixed fee, contingent fee, hourly fee). Review the appropriate contract with your client, including the services to be rendered by you, your client's responsibilities, and your fee schedule. If your client is to provide you with a retainer, that is discussed as well.

iii. Ask Your Client to Commit to You

Now that your client knows that you will accept the case and what this representation will cost, your client has the opportunity to hire or not hire you. Your client may have found relief in the fact that the story has been told to an impartial third person and once considering the costs of going forward, now believes that nothing further needs be done. Or your client may have begun the bonding process with you and consents to your attorney/client contract for services. If the latter, the attorney/client relationship is created and the prospective client is transformed into your client.

d. Proposing a Solution or a Strategy for Resolving the Problem

Under the ABA/LSD *Client Counseling Competition Rules and Standards for Judging*, the consultation includes both a complete interview and some counseling. In the counseling portion of the consultation, you are to "propose a solution or other means of resolving the problem." This involves two components: (1) the array of processes that could be employed for resolving the problem; and (2) the legal and nonlegal solutions of the problem. At times the processes and the solutions become intertwined (*i.e.*, the process dictates the solution).

When preparing for the consultation, first consider all the alternative processes of dispute resolution. The alternatives should include a number of ADR strategies and litigation, as well as a number of non-traditional processes. Consider which processes are available to your client and which are available to the other party?

Remember that the consultation is only thirty minutes. Therefore, plan to spend only a few minutes on proposing a solution or a strategy for resolving the problem. You will have additional time to discuss this segment in the post-consultation.

i. Develop an Array of ADR Processes Plus Litigation

The range of dispute resolution processes forms a continuum beginning with the least intrusive where one disputant resolves the dispute through unilateral action to the most intrusive where one or both parties invite a third party to resolve the dispute for them. The continuum includes:

- inaction
- acquiescence
- self-help
- negotiation

- ombudsmanship (corporate, institution, and government sponsored)
- mediation (private and court-sponsored)
- arbitration (private and court-annexed)
- litigation (court and private judging)

Inaction

Inaction is the most common form of dispute resolution. Since a dispute requires at least two participants, if one party does not pursue the other, the dispute is resolved.

Acquiescence

Acquiescence is another common form of dispute resolution. If one party gives in to the other's demands, the dispute is resolved.

Self-Help

Self-help, another form of unilateral action as a method of dispute resolution, is the opposite of inaction. Inaction is passive; self-help is active. Inaction abandons rights; self-help asserts rights.

The Uniform Commercial Code, for example, provides a number of self-help remedies. Some buyers who receive nonconforming goods may reject them or may deduct all or any part of the damages from the price. A secured party may repossess collateral if the debtor defaults. In some non-UCC transactions, a party may refuse to perform if the other contracting party had a duty to perform first and has failed to do so.

Negotiation

Negotiation is a voluntary, consensual, private dispute resolution process. Unlike inaction, acquiescence, and self-help where a party acts unilaterally, the parties in negotiation must work together to resolve their dispute. They do not involve a third party to either direct the discussion or resolve the dispute for them.

Ombudsmanship

Ombudsmanship adds a third party to the dispute resolution process. An ombudsman, as the concept developed in the United States in the 1960s, is a member of the management team of a public or private organization. The ombudsman, through investigation and informal counseling, helps resolve organizational related disputes confidentially and before they develop into lawsuits. The ombudsman can also alert upper management of major problems as they are arising. Management may then gain insight into ways to resolve these problems and take corrective action before these problems reach the litigation stage and become much more difficult to address.

Ombudsmanship has broad application. For example, corporations employ ombudsmen to investigate employee complaints, hospitals and nursing homes use ombudsmen to investigate patient complaints, and colleges and universities use ombudsmen to investigate student complaints.

The ombudsman need not be corporate or industry appointed. The ombudsman may be government sponsored. For example, on the federal level, ombudsmanship offices include a Taxpayer Ombudsman of the Internal Revenue Service, a Student Financial Assistance Ombudsman, the Small Business and Agriculture Regulatory Enforcement Ombudsman, FDIC Office of the Ombudsman, and the CDER Ombudsman.

On the state level, ombudsmanship offices have become a regular feature of government. It is common to see an Ombudsman for Injured Workers, a Long Term Care Ombudsman, an Ombudsman for Mental Health and Mental Retardation, an Office of Taxpayer Ombudsman, and a more general Ombudsman-Citizens' Aide.

Mediation

Mediation, like ombudsmanship, adds a third party to the dispute resolution process. In mediation, the third party neutral is invited to participate in the process but not in the decision making. Mediation has traditionally been a private consensual process. This means that either prior to or during the dispute, the parties decide that before pursuing litigation, the parties should use mediation to try to resolve their dispute. Since mediation is a private process, the procedural and evidentiary rules of the process are those agreed to by the disputants. The parties may fashion their own rules or they may agree to have the mediator determine the rules for them.

The mediator facilitates the discussion between the parties in an attempt to help the parties resolve their dispute. The mediator controls only the process and the parties negotiate through the mediator. The mediator does not resolve the dispute. If the role of the mediator is only facilitative, the mediator will refrain from proposing solutions. The facilitative mediator will only assist the parties in focusing their discussion on the nature of their problem, their interests, and the array of resolutions they suggest. Some mediators will go beyond being merely faciliative and will add their own evaluation. They will evaluate the problem and propose solutions. Even if the mediator proposes solutions, the parties ultimately must resolve their own dispute.

Although traditionally mediation has been a private process (the parties hire and pay the mediator), in recent years a number of courts have added mediation to the litigation process. If the mediator is a judge, magistrate judge, or adjunct settlement judge, the process may be called a settlement conference. In a court-sponsored or court-ordered settlement conference, the litigants agree to participate in the process before they have an opportunity to appear in court to litigate their dispute. The settlement conference is conducted by a neutral third party (judge, magistrate judge, or court appointed adjunct settlement judge) and is held in private at the courthouse. The neutral party may or may not have been selected because of a specialized subject expertise. A judge not wearing a robe sitting at a conference table with the litigants and their attorneys contrasts nicely with the judge in a robe sitting behind an elevated bench in a formal courtroom.

The settlement conference is informal but structured by the settlement judge. The proceedings give the attorneys for each litigant an opportunity to explore the factors that might lead to settlement. These factors include: the legal aspects of the dispute; the extent of the injury (and how sympathetic the victim will look at trial); a defendant's ability to pay a judgment or settlement; the cost of litigation; the home town aspects of the case (whether a local litigant will have an advantage over an out of towner); the attractiveness of the parties and the witnesses to the jury; the fairness of the result; and the individual concerns of the parties. If settlement is not reached, the settlement conference can be used to establish timetables and streamline the issues for trial. If settlement is achieved, a mutually acceptable agreement is attained. The agreement is the litigants' agreement and not a resolution imposed by the settlement judge. The agreement need not parallel the "legal" resolution of the dispute before the court.

Arbitration

Arbitration is at the intrusive end of the dispute resolution spectrum. In arbitration, the disputants come before a third party, the arbitrator, relate the nature of their dispute to the arbitrator, and the arbitrator resolves the dispute. Since the third party resolves the dispute, the disputants have lost control over the outcome of their dispute.

Arbitration has traditionally been a private consensual process. This means that either prior to or during the dispute, the disputants decide that the dispute should be resolved by an arbitrator. Since arbitration is a private process, the procedural and evidentiary rules of the process are those agreed to by the disputants. Rather than fashion their own rules, the disputants may agree to have the arbitrator determine the rules for them.

In the 1980s, Congress funded ten federal district courts to experiment with mandatory programs of court-annexed arbitration as part of the public adjudication process. In 1988, Congress authorized the continuation of these mandatory pilot programs and authorized additional voluntary pilot programs. In the mid 1990s, the number of federal court-annexed arbitration programs dwindled until the number of active programs decreased to five by the turn of the century.

An industry may set up arbitration as the process for resolved disputes among its members. For example, in professional baseball, final offer arbitration (baseball arbitration) is used for salary disputes between players and owners.

Litigation

Litigation is at the most intrusive end of the dispute resolution spectrum. Litigation may proceed through a public (governmental) forum—a court—or before a privately created forum—a rent-a-judge (private judging). Litigation in a court is initiated by one of the parties who becomes the plaintiff. The other party involuntarily becomes the defendant. The procedural and evidentiary rules of the court apply to this dispute and to these litigants as well as to all disputes and all litigants coming before this court.

In litigation, the disputants come before a third party or third parties, depending on whether the case is being tried before a judge (as the trier of the law) and jury (as the trier of the facts) or only before a judge (as the trier of both the law and the facts). Through a formal presentation of evidence, choreographed by the litigants' attorneys, the litigants' case is presented to the trier of the facts and the trier of the law who resolve the dispute. The decision of the trial court may be appealed to a higher court but again it will be third parties who resolve the dispute. Since the third parties have resolved the dispute, the litigants have lost control over the outcome of their dispute.

Parties have experimented with private judging or rent-a-judge as part of the private adjudication process. If the private judging is by contract the parties must negotiate the procedural and evidentiary rules as well as the extent of pretrial discovery, whether the trial will be before a judge and jury or only a judge, who will be the judge, who will pay the judge and how much, where and when the trial will be held, how long the trial will last, and whether the judge's decision will be advisory or binding. If the private judging is by court reference (court appointment) (about half of the states permit the court to appoint a private judge to handle a specific case), the court's evidentiary rules and procedures will be followed unless the parties modify the rules and procedures. In private litigation, the parties' attorneys choreograph the presentation of facts and law and the third party (the private judge) resolves the dispute. The dispute is resolved according to "the law." If the private judging is by contract, the decision may or may not be binding, depending on what the parties had decided. A binding decision cannot be appealed. If the private judging is by court reference, the decision is binding and may be appealed within the judicial system.

ii. Develop an Arsenal of Non-Traditional Methods

In addition to the ADR methods of dispute resolution plus litigation, consider expanding the client's options by including several non-traditional processes. Be creative. For example, if your client's company is charged with sexual harassment, it could offer an apology, back pay, revision of the employment manual, an internal investigation, professional job placement service, or placement under a different supervisor. If your client was involved in an automobile accident and owns an automobile dealership, your client could offer to repair the other person's vehicle or replace the vehicle with one from the dealership's used car lot. If your client's company is having difficulty performing under a contract, your client could offer to modify the contract to meet the other party's needs while making it possible for your client to perform. Once the concept of a non-traditional process (which in itself may be the solution) is presented at the consultation, your client may add other methods (or solutions) to the spectrum of possibilities.

iii. Develop Advantages and Disadvantages for Each Dispute Resolution Process

Each dispute resolution process has advantages and disadvantages. What may be an advantage to one party may be a disadvantage to another. For example, a party who seeks reimbursement for medical expenses views time as an enemy while the insurance company views time as an ally. The claimant needs prompt payment while the insurance company makes money by delaying payment.

The following are some attributes that should be considered with regard to each dispute resolution process:

- time necessary to resolve the dispute
- transaction costs to resolve the dispute
- personal costs involved to resolve the dispute
- degree of risk in an adverse resolution
- degree of control in fashioning the ultimate resolution
- publicity involved during the resolution process
- publicity of the outcome
- finality and when
- need to maintain or enhance a continuing relationship

For a more detailed discussion of the various methods of dispute resolution and their advantages and disadvantages, see Martin A. Frey, *Does ADR Offer Second Class Justice?*, 36 Tulsa Law Journal 727 (Summer 2001), and Martin A. Frey, *Representing Clients Effectively in an ADR Environment*, 33 Tulsa Law Journal 443 (Fall 1997).

Based on these and other attributes and considering your client's position in the dispute, develop a series of charts listing the advantages and disadvantages for each method of dispute resolution. Note that what may be an advantage to one party may be a disadvantage to another. Whether something is an advantage or disadvantage depends on one's goals. In the previous example, an insurance company will believe that a lengthy process works in its favor because it delays the time, if ever, the insurance company will be required to pay the claimant. On the other hand, a claimant will view a lengthy process as a disadvantage because he or she may need the money to pay medical bills and provide income for day to day living expenses. With this in mind, a hypothetical chart for litigation and a hypothetical chart for mediation could take the following form for the claimant.

LITIGATION
(claimant's chart)

ADVANTAGES	*DISADVANTAGES*
a decision is rendered at the end of the process	substantial time to reach the end of the process
finality at the end of the process	may involve appeals prior to finality
the decision is by an impartial third party	litigants do not participate in fashioning the decision

the decision based on the law and the facts	decision not based on business or personal factors
if the trial court renders an adverse decision, the trial judge's decision as to the law is subject to judicial review	substantial transaction costs; in some cases, the losing party may be required to pay the winning party's attorney fees
public process and neither the process nor the judgment are confidential	one party wins and the other loses
even if the litigation process is initiated, over 90% of the cases filed are settled by a process other than litigation	time consuming and personally draining
the winning party receives a judgment but may need to execute on the judgment to satisfy it	

MEDIATION
(claimant's chart)

ADVANTAGES	_DISADVANTAGES_
the decision is by the parties	the facts and the law do not control the outcome
the parties can fashion an agreement that meets their own special needs	the process does not guarantee a level playing field (one party may be able to take advantage of the other during the mediation)
a neutral third party directs the discussion but does not resolve the dispute for the parties	if the parties cannot agree, there is no resolution at the end of the process
quick	
the parties control the timetable	
limited transaction costs	
as a part of the mediation,	

the parties may determine who
pays the transaction costs

the mediation may produce a
win/win result

because the parties have
fashioned their own agreement
that meets their respective
needs, the likelihood is that
the agreement will be performed

iv. Develop Questions that Focus Client's Attention on the Attributes of the Various Dispute Resolution Processes

Based on these attributes for the various dispute resolution processes, develop a list of general questions that will provide your client with an opportunity to discuss each attribute. For example, if your client is a doctor being sued for medical malpractice, these questions could take the following form:

- How much are you willing to spend in the process of having this dispute resolved?
- What do you foresee as the costs of this dispute to you personally, to you professionally, and to your family?
- What degree of risk can you assume of an adverse resolution?
- How much control would you want in fashioning the ultimate resolution?
- How much publicity can you tolerate as this dispute is being resolved?
- How much publicity can you tolerate as a result of an adverse resolution?

Avoid questions that deal specifically with a dispute resolution process such as "How do you feel about litigation?" This type of question prejudges a process. Your task here is limited to understanding how your client feels about some of the attributes of the various processes. You may discover that your client likes some of the attributes of one process and dislikes other attributes of this same process. Ultimately, the client may be required to compromise in his or her selection of a process. Generally, no one process will give your client all the advantages he or she seeks and at the same time not give your client any of the disadvantages.

e. *Wrapping Up*

Wrapping up the consultation involves two steps: assigning tasks and scheduling the hypothetical counseling session.

i. *Assign Tasks*

Now that the attorney/client relationship has been formed and a solution or process has been proposed for resolving the problem, plans must be set in motion for implementing what has been discussed. Before you can begin to implement the agreed upon course of action or begin to plan for the hypothetical counseling session (a much more detailed session than the quick counseling held during the consultation), you must have all the relevant information that your client has. You may have had some success in obtaining documents and other tangible information from your client during the gathering facts and feelings segment of the consultation. If, during the consultation, you learned that your client has information that was not brought to the session, ask your client to bring this additional information to you. All this information must be considered by you before you can move forward in your client's case. Establish a date certain for delivery of this information to you. A written list of what the client should bring and the date due should be given to the client and a copy included in the client's file.

ii. *Schedule the Hypothetical Counseling Session, If One Is Necessary*

As the last event of the consultation, you should schedule the appointment for the hypothetical counseling session, if such a session is necessary. You should also inform your client what will happen and when it will happen in the client's case. Do not promise results.

After the date and time for a future meeting is established, assuming a future meeting is necessary, you should escort your client to the exit.

For a more detailed discussion of interviewing and counseling, *see* Robert M. Bastress & Joseph D. Harbaugh, INTERVIEWING, COUNSELING, AND NEGOTIATING: SKILLS FOR EFFECTIVE REPRESENTATION chs. 4&10 (1990).

B. The Post-Consultation

In the ABA/LSD Client Counseling Competition, the client will leave the room after the thirty minute consultation. You now have fifteen minutes for the post-consultation. If the consultation exceeds thirty minutes, your time for the post-consultation will be reduced accordingly. The post-consultation is extremely important because it gives you an opportunity to highlight what you were trying to accomplish during the consultation and it gives you an opportunity to discuss as a team in the presence of the judges what you will do to prepare for the more extensive counseling session and other services that need to be performed to represent your client. The judges will only observe during the post-consultation; they have been instructed not to ask you questions. Fifteen minutes is not a long time so use your time efficiently.

The ABA/LSD *Client Counseling Competition Rules and Standards for Judging* art. XI.B. describes the post-consultation. During the post-consultation consider:

1. discussing the consultation—what you had planned to do, why you had planned to do it, whether you were able to do what you planned, and what you would do differently

2. discussing how you worked as a team

3. dictating a memorandum to the file summarizing the consultation, describing the scope of the legal work to be undertaken, stating the legal issues that will need to be researched

4. dictating a letter to the client confirming the attorney/client relationship (including the fee arrangement, the client's responsibilities, and the next appointment), a letter to opposing counsel, or a letter to the party with whom the client is having their legal problems

Remember, you have only fifteen minutes for the post-consultation so prepare in advance and be organized.

C. The Judges' Grading of the Consultation and Post-Consultation

The ABA/LSD *Client Counseling Competition Evaluation Form* asks the judges to evaluate a team's performance in ten areas:

1. Working Atmosphere

   How effectively did the team establish a working atmosphere and an attorney/client relationship with its client?

   Was the consultation conducted in a courteous, sensitive and professional manner?

   Did the team inform its client as to the duration, purpose, and overview of the consultation?

   Did the team discuss the special nature of the attorney/client relationship, including confidentiality, fees, mutual rights and obligations, and availability?

2. Problem Description

   How effectively did the team learn how its client viewed his or her situation?

   Was the team able to elicit both facts and the client's feelings?

   Did the team develop a reasonably complete and accurate description of the problem?

3. Client's Goals

   How effectively did the team learn its client's goals and expectations?

   Was the team able to refine its client's goals and expectations?

4. Problem Analysis

   How effectively did the team analyzed its client's problems?

   Did the team demonstrate creativity when analyzing its client's problem?

   Did the team analyze its client's problem from both a legal and nonlegal perspective?

   Did the team arrive at a clear and useful formulation of the client's problem?

5. Moral/Ethical Issues

   How effectively did the team recognize and address any moral or ethical issues that arose during the consultation?

   Did the team deal with these issue in a nonjudgmental and prejudicial manner?

6. Alternative Courses of Action

   How effectively did the team develop alternative solutions?

Were the alternatives both legal and nonlegal?

Were these alternatives potentially effective and feasible?

7. Client's Informed Choice

How effectively did the team assist its client in understanding and making informed choices among possible courses of action?

When assisting its client in making an informed choice, were the potential legal, economic, social, and psychological consequences taken into consideration?

8. Effective Conclusion

How effectively did the team conclude the consultation?

Was the consultation concluded skillfully?

Did the client leave the consultation with a clear understanding of what his or her obligations were and what the attorney's obligations were?

Did the client leave the consultation with reasonable expectations?

Did the client leave the consultation feeling reasonably confident that his or her attorneys would represent his or her interests?

9. Teamwork

How effectively did the team work together and how effectively did they balance participation?

Did the team show good chemistry?

Did the members of the team demonstrate flexible as to their roles?

Did the members of the team collaborate in the consultation?

10. Post-Consultation Reflections

How effectively did the team analyze the consultation and its client's problems?

Did the members of the team analyze whether they recognized their own and their client's feelings?

Did they analyze whether they recognized the strengths and limitations of their interviewing and counseling skills?

Did they analyze whether they recognized the strengths and limitations of their handling the legal and nonlegal aspects of their client's substantive problem?

For each of the ten questions, each judge of the three judge panel ranks on the basis of an "a," "b," "c," "d," and "e" scale. An "a" means "highly effective" and is equivalent to "1." An "e" means "very ineffective" and is equivalent to "5." By totaling the scores on the 10 questions, each judge arrives at a score for the team. The judges repeat the process for each team. After the three judge panel has seen their three teams, each judge will rank the teams 1, 2, 3. This process will be repeated for the first three rounds. After the three rounds have been completed, the three teams with the lowest total scores will advance to the final round.

Chapter 5

Negotiating for Your Client

This chapter on negotiating discusses skills for the Negotiation Competition. Generally a negotiation competition will involve three rounds with all teams (two students per team) participating in the first two rounds. The four teams with the lowest scores advance to the third and final round. This assumes that the competition is scaled so the lower the score, the better the performance.

Prior to the competition, all teams receive a set of general facts for all three rounds. Each team also receives confidential facts for the first two rounds of the competition. After the first two rounds are completed, the four teams advancing to the final round will receive confidential facts for that round. The rules for the American Bar Association's Law Student Division Negotiation Competition are found at *http://www.abanet. org/lsd.*

The actual negotiation in a negotiation competition is very dynamic. Each team can only guess the confidential facts of the other side. In a negotiation competition, both members of a team play the role of attorneys. Since the client is not present, the attorneys cannot caucus with the client during the negotiation. They may, however, caucus between themselves. They can only guess what the client would say. The fact that a team has only the general facts and the confidential facts for its side does not mean that little preparation is required. The key to a good performance is preparation.

A. Preparing for the Negotiation

A negotiation, by its very name, is two sided — your side and the other side. Therefore, as you prepare, visualize both your side and the other side.

1. Investigate the Facts and Research the Law

Based on the general and confidential facts, investigate the facts and research the applicable law. Investigating the facts requires you to do more than review the facts given you. You may want to be creative and search for additional facts. A good, quick source of information is the internet. If the problem deals with solar panels, then an internet search on solar panels may prove informative. You may want to check for judicial opinions on Westlaw or Lexus to see whether your client or the client on the other side has been involved in litigation and, if so, with what result. An investigation of the facts also requires consideration of the parties' feelings. Often, a party's feelings drive a dispute.

Depending on the problem, you may or may not be required to research the law. Often, in a negotiation competition, the central problem will be how much a person will be paid or which divisions of which companies will be downsized if two companies merge.

Researching the law requires the determination of possible causes of action. These causes of action may be those that your client could initiate or those that the other party could initiate. Could the facts present an action, for example, for negligence, strict liability, defamation, breach of contract, or sexual harassment? Or could the facts present an action based on statute, such as, the Uniform Commercial Code, state lemon law, RICO, an unfair labor practice, or an antitrust violation? For each possibility, the precedent must be found, assuming precedent does exist.

2. Apply the Law to the Facts

Once the facts have been developed and the applicable law researched, you must develop an understanding of how the law applies to the facts. For each cause of action, the elements must be isolated and the facts must be applied to each element. If your client's problem were to be litigated, what would be the strengths and weaknesses in your client's position as to each element of each cause of action? Once this analysis has been concluded, you will have a pretty good idea of what your client's legal position would be.

3. Define the Problem

Defining the problem requires you to define the problem both from your client's perspective and from the other party's perspective. As you define the problem you may discover not one but two problems—how your client defines the problem and how the other party defines the problem.

For example, in the real estate market, the owner of a house may view her problem as selling her home quickly for the maximum price that could be realized. A potential buyer may view his problem as buying a house to satisfy specific needs. Or an employer may view its problem as needing a employee to perform unique and essential services for the company. A perspective employee may view her problem as finding a position that accommodates her lifestyle.

The previous examples describe problems that are not disputes. The parties are attempting to create new relationships. On the other hand, problems can take the form of disputes. For example, Stephanie Emerson, a teller at First Bank, claims that she was approached by the branch manager who told her that if she would provide him with sexual favors, he would see to it that she would be promoted to head teller. Stephanie responded by filing a sexual harassment charge with the EEOC against the branch manager and the bank. The branch manager asserts that he never made the statements.

4. Identify the Parties' Interests

Identify the parties' interests. "Why" does a party want a certain outcome? Remember to identify the interests of both your client and the other party. Your client will never consent to an agreement if his or her interests have not been satisfied. The other party will also never consent to the agreement if his or her interests have not been satisfied. Generally, it is impossible to satisfy all the interests of both parties. The primary interests of both parties must be satisfied for there to be a negotiated agreement.

5. Identify a Range of Possible Solutions

Create a list of possible solutions and commit these solution to paper. Begin by articulating a solution that would be the most favorable to your client. Then articulate a solution that would be the most favorable to the other party. It should be readily apparent that your client will not accept the solution that is most favorable to the other party because it would not meet your client's interests (although it would possibly satisfy all of the other party's interests). It should also be readily apparent that the other party will not accept the solution that is most favorable to your client because it would not meet that party's interests (although it would possibly satisfy all of your client's interests). You have, by this exercise established the two extreme positions for the negotiation. An agreement, however, will not be reached if only the interests of one party will be met. Both parties must come away from the bargaining table feeling that at least some of their interests have been met. Therefore, create a range of possible solutions between these two extreme positions. Try to develop solutions that will meet not only your client's interests but also those of the other party.

The following worksheet will help you define the problem(s), interests, and range of possible solutions:

Worksheet for Dissecting the Content of the Negotiation

Defining the Problem(s)

Defining the Problem from
Your Client's Perspective

Defining the Problem from
the Other Party's Perspective

Identifying Interests

Your Client's Interests

The Other Party's Interests

Possible Solutions

Solution Most Favorable
to Your Client

Meets the Following Interests
of Your Client

Does Not Meet the Following
Interests of Your Client

Meets the Following Interests
of the Other Side

Does Not Meet the Following
<u>Interests of the Other Side</u>

Solution Most Favorable
<u>to the Other Side</u>

Meets the Following Interests
<u>of Your Client</u>

Does Not Meet the Following
<u>Interests of Your Client</u>

Meets the Following Interests
<u>of the Other Side</u>

Does Not Meet the Following
<u>Interests of the Other Side</u>

Possible Solution #3

Meets the Following Interests
<u>of Your Client</u>

Does Not Meet the Following
<u>Interests of Your Client</u>

Meets the Following Interests
<u>of the Other Side</u>

Does Not Meet the Following
<u>Interests of the Other Side</u>

Possible Solution #4

Meets the Following Interests
<u>of Your Client</u>

Does Not Meet the Following
<u>Interests of Your Client</u>

Meets the Following Interests
<u>of the Other Side</u>

Does Not Meet the Following
<u>Interests of the Other Side</u>

6. Selecting a Negotiation Strategy

Now that you have dissected the problem, the interests, and possible solutions, and have evaluated these solutions against your interests and the other party's interests, it is time to decide upon your negotiation strategy. The following discussion focuses on two strategies: position based negotiation and interest based negotiation.

Traditionally, negotiations have been position (solution) based. In position based negotiation the parties state their positions (solutions) and negotiate from those positions. Each tries to convince the other to change position. As the negotiation evolves, the parties focus on "distributing a fixed pie" rather than on "expanding the pie." Both parties cannot have their interests equally met and thus position based negotiation results in a solution whereby one party *wins* more than the other party. What one party gets, the other gives up.

Interest based negotiation focuses on the parties interests and a range of solutions. It is not constructed around the single solution (or position) offered by each party. In this way, the parties can create new solutions to meet their similar and different interests. As a part of the process, the parties focus on "expanding the pie" rather than "distributing a fixed pie." Both parties can have their basic interests met and thus interest based negotiation leads to a solution whereby both parties *win*. This approach moves the parties from a "win/lose" mode to "win/win."

a. *Position Based Negotiation*

Position based (distributive) negotiation, as its name denotes, requires the parties to begin by stating their positions or solutions. For planning purposes, however, position based negotiators should know three positions, rather than just one. They should know their opening position, their most extreme position (*e.g.*, the highest they would pay if they are the buyer or the lowest they would accept if they are the seller), and their target position (*i.e.*, what they really want).

For example, assume that Tom and Misty Lopez own a house that they would like to sell. Before they put their house on the market, they should know three numbers. The first is their target price. This is the amount they would like to receive for their house. To arrive at this number, they have investigated what other comparable houses in their neighborhood have sold for over the past year. The second is the minimum amount they would take for their house. This depends on their financial situation, the market, and the urgency in which they need to sell their house. The third number is their opening price. They can calculate this by comparing what other sellers in their neighborhood have opened with, how long their houses were on the market, and the actual selling price. If the Lopezes had opened at their target price, it would be unlikely that they could sell their house without dropping some amount off of their price. Therefore, they gave themselves little opportunity to receive their target price.

The following is a planning tool for position based negotiation:

Position Based (Distributive) Negotiation Worksheet

Identify your own opening offer, target, and lowest or opening counteroffer, target, maximum.

Can you predict the other side's three numbers?

one side	scale	other side
opening offer____	____	_
_	____	_
_	____	_
_	____	_
target ____	____	_
_	____	_
_	____	_
_	____	_
_	____	_
lowest ____	____	_
_	____	_
_	____	_
_	____	_
_	____	____ maximum
_	____	_
_	____	_
_	____	_
_	____	_
_	____	____ target
_	____	_
_	____	_
_	____	_
	____	____opening counteroffer

Reasons why the other side should change their position	Their response to your reasons
(1)	
(2)	
(3)	
(4)	

Reasons posed by the other side why you should change your position	Your response to their reasons
(1)	
(2)	
(3)	
(4)	

In a position based negotiation, a negotiated agreement cannot be reached until there is some overlap between the opening offer and lowest on the part of one party and the opening counteroffer and maximum of the other. This overlap creates a settlement zone. That is, the parties will negotiate an agreement somewhere in this overlap area. When the negotiations first open, generally the parties have no settlement zone. As the parties tug and push each other, one party's bottom line will descend and the other party's maximum will ascend. If enough movement occurs, a settlement zone will be created and the parties will arrive at an agreement.

For example, return to Tom and Misty Lopez and their house that they would like to sell. Before they put their house on the market, they have determined the following. They have investigated the sale price of other comparable houses in their neighborhood and have calculated their target price to be $225,000. Second, they have determined the minimum amount they would take for their house, $200,000. Third, they have established their opening price at $250,000.

Richard and Mary Ellen O'Connor have been looking for a house in the school district in which the Lopez house is located. Their realtor has shown them the Lopez house. The O'Connors open with an offer (really a counteroffer) of $185,000. Although the Lopezes do not know it, the O'Connors have a target of $210,000 and are willing to go as high as $235,000.

Tom and Misty Lopez   Richard and Mary Ellen O'Connor

$250,000........

.............................$235,000...............

.   .

. $225,000........   .

.   .

.   ...$210,000   .

.   .

...$200,000...

........$185,000

The settlement zone is between $200,000 and $235,000. The house should sell to the O'Connors at somewhere between these two numbers. The settlement zone is dynamic because the parties may change their numbers as the negotiation continues. Often there is no settlement zone when the negotiation begins but one develops as the negotiation continues.

b. Interest Based Negotiation

An interest based negotiation can be structured in four segments — defining the problem(s) to be negotiated, identifying the interests of the parties (the clients), creating and evaluating solutions against the parties' interests, and drafting the agreement. "The Worksheet for Dissecting the Content of the Negotiation" provides the planning for interest based negotiation.

B. Executing Your Plan at the Negotiation

Bring a step by step outline of your plan to the negotiation. The execution of your plan requires you keep with your format. The first step will be the same regardless of whether your strategy is to use position based negotiation or interest based negotiation. The first step is to define the problem that is under discussion at this negotiation. Does the other side see the problem the same way or do they have a different problem to resolve? Listen carefully to what the other side has to say about the problem. After the problem is defined, the structure of the negotiation will differ depending on whether you have selected position based negotiation or interest based negotiation.

1. Position Based Negotiation

If you have selected position based negotiation as your strategy, now make your opening offer. Be prepared to counter the other side's criticism of your opening offer. The other side will begin with a litany of reasons why your offer is unreasonable.

If the other side preempts you and states their opening offer first, you have the opportunity to criticize the reasonableness of their offer. After the challenges and counter challenges have been voiced, make your counteroffer and be prepared for the other side's criticism. Structure your offer and counteroffers so you move toward your target counteroffer.

2. Interest Based Negotiation

If you have selected interest based negotiation as your strategy, then (after the discussion of the problem) move to a discussion of interests. If the other side wants to make an offer and thus use position based negotiation, do not criticize their offer and do not make a counteroffer. Stick to your strategy and bring the discussion around to their interests and your interests. If the other side makes an offer, ask what interests their offer satisfies. If the inquiry of "interests" proves unproductive, ask "why" they like their offer. "What" does their offer accomplish?

a. Discuss Interests

Discuss your client's interests and also discuss the other client's interests. Check your "Worksheet for Dissecting the Content of the Negotiation" to see whether your perceptions of the other client's interests were correct. The interests of both parties must be understood for there to be a negotiated agreement. Do not try to dissuade the other side about their interests. Understand their interests; do not challenge their interests as unreasonable.

Write down the interests as they are being discussed. You may want three columns: my client's interests, mutual interests, and your client's interests. You may also want to discuss the priority of interests. Which interests are primary and which are secondary?

In the Lopez/O'Connor example, it might be helpful to ask the O'-Connors what they like about the Lopez house. Their answers might include the neighborhood, the size of the house, the location to schools, the condition of the house, and the location to shopping. They may also like the fact that interests rates are low so they could buy more house for the same monthly payments.

At the end of the discussion of interests, review your written list of interests. Ask whether any interests have been omitted from the list. Double check your Worksheet. If an interest has been omitted, it should be discussed and added to the written list.

b. Create and Discuss a Range of Solutions

Following the summary of the list of interests, the parties should focus on developing a list of possible solutions to the problem(s). The process should be a collaborative effort. The list of possible solutions should not be "my list" and "your list" but rather "our list." This phase of the process should begin by the parties understanding that the list is merely a list for discussion purposes and nothing has been decided. If the other party has already made an offer, list the offer as one of the possible solutions. The Worksheet will provide you with ideas for possible solutions to add to the common list. The common list should be developed collaboratively rather than one side reading a laundry list of possibilities.

As the list is being developed, both sides should refrain from evaluating an item on the list. Only when the list is complete should the possible solutions be evaluated against the interests list. If a possible solution is prematurely evaluated, the list of possible solutions will not be fully developed and the negotiation will veer toward position based negotiation rather than staying the course with interest based negotiation. Only after all the possible solutions have been evaluated against the interests list should the discussion focus on the possible solution or solutions that accommodates both parties's interests.

For a more detailed discussion of interest based negotiation, *see* Roger Fisher, William Ury & Bruce Patton, GETTING TO YES (2d ed. 1991).

c. Drafting the Agreement

After the solution or combination of solutions that best meets the parties's interests has been selected, the agreement must be reduced to a writing. The writing should be as complete as possible. Details omitted from the writing will cause the contract to unravel.

For example, LouAnn and George Polaski had three children before their divorce. Prior to their divorce, the parties agreed upon custody and visitation. LouAnn was to have custody of the children, George would have unlimited visitation rights, and the children were to visit their father on two holidays a year. All went well until the first Christmas after the divorce. George wanted the children to visit him so he could take them to Disney World. LouAnn wanted the children to stay with her so they would be with her parents on Christmas Day. Although LouAnn and George had agreed upon two holidays a year, the writing did not designate which holidays were under the visitation plan or how the holiday determination was to be made.

Also remember that under the parol evidence rule, a contract may have two components: a written component (*i.e.*, the integration or final writing) and a parol component (*i.e.*, the non integrated writings and oral terms). A document that includes all the terms in detail will diminish a subsequent challenge that the writing is not a total integration.

Both sides should read and correct the writing before either side signs. If the writing is drafted before the other side had read and consented to it, the other side may have corrections, additions, or deletions, that will need to be initialed by the parties. By waiting to sign until both sides have read and agreed upon the accuracy and completeness of the writing, one signature without initialing per party would be sufficient.

If an attorney who is negotiating on behalf of a client does not have the authority to accept the agreement, the terms of the agreement cannot be finalized at that moment. The attorney must, in good faith, present the tentative agreement to the client and recommend the client's acceptance. Before the attorney leaves the negotiation, the attorney should initial the agreement with the understanding that the agreement will be presented to the client for acceptance by a date certain.

Before the negotiation has concluded, both sides should have a copy of the signed agreement. Only one version of the agreement should be signed and dated. If each attorney makes a draft of the agreement, the versions may differ, however slightly, and this may lead to a subsequent dispute.

The following tips may help you draft a better contract.

1. Create an outline for the contract and draft from this outline. An outline will help you present the terms of the contract in a logical, orderly fashion. An outline prevents the omission or duplication of essential terms.

2. Begin the writing by defining the purpose of the contract.

3. Organize the contract by grouping similar items together (*e.g.*, group the duties of one party and then group the duties of the other party).

4. Be brief. Omit surplus words, sentences and paragraphs. State the meaning clearly and concisely. Wordiness only creates an opportunity for ambiguity and confusion.

5. Use clear, concise terms. Avoid synonyms. Do not confuse the reader by using different words to refer to the same thing.

6. Avoid legalese. Legalese only makes a writing pompous and confusing. Minimize confusion by referring to the parties by name rather than "the party of the first part."

7. Avoid indefinite pronouns such as "it, they, this, who, and which." Indefinite pronouns only add confusion. When possible substitute a noun for a pronoun.

8. Avoid "etc." Etc. adds no new content.

9. Avoid sexist language.

For further discussion, *see* Martin A. Frey & Phyllis Hurley Frey, ESSENTIALS OF CONTRACT LAW ch. 6 (Delmar-West Legal Studies 2000).

C. Self-Analysis

Just when you think the negotiation is over, you discover one more stage — the self-analysis. Preparation for the self-analysis is extremely important because this is the last time the judges will see you before they complete their grading and this is the only time the judges will see you when the other side is not present. Therefore, this is your opportunity to leave a lasting impression.

Under the ABA/LSD rules, each team has ten minutes for the self-analysis. Each team should open the self-analysis by addressing the following questions:

1. In reflecting on the entire negotiation, if you faced a similar situation tomorrow, what would you do the same and what would you do differently?

2. How well did your strategy work in relation to the outcome?

From our point of view, the questions appear to be presented in reverse order. It would seem more appropriate to begin by discussing your strategy and your desired solution (outcome). Compare your desired outcome with the actual outcome of the negotiation session. This can then be followed by "how well your strategy worked in relation to the outcome." Then address the "what would you do the same and what would you do differently" question.

As with the negotiation itself, both members of the team should participate in the self-analysis. Students should be prepared to be interrupted by the judges.

Your preparation for the negotiation competition requires you not only to plan for the negotiation (see section A), but also to execute the plan in practice rounds before mock judges (with Evaluation Criteria Forms). We suggest that each practice negotiation end with the self-critique. The self-critique, along with the negotiation itself, can then be critiqued by the mock judges.

D. The Judges' Grading of the Negotiation Session

The judges instructions for the American Bar Association's Law Student Division Negotiation Competition state:

> The evaluation criteria form scales themselves attempt to divide what is recognized as a dynamic and complicated process into discrete components and attributes that should be present in any approach to negotiation....

> These standards are also based on the premise that there is no one "correct" approach to effective negotiation in all circumstances. Instead, the strategies and techniques used will vary with the nature of the problem, the specific mix of personalities involved, and other circumstances. Whatever approach is used, however, negotiation effectiveness can be judged at least in part by its <u>outcome</u>. A good negotiation outcome is one that:

> Is better than the best alternative to a negotiated agreement (with <u>this</u> party)

> Satisfies the interests of:

> > the client—very well

> > the other side—acceptably (enough for them to agree and follow through)

> > third parties—tolerably (so they won't disrupt the agreement)

Adopts a solution that is the best of all available options

Is legitimate—no one feels "taken"

Involves commitments that are clear and realistic

Involves communication that is efficient and well-understood, and

Results in an enhanced working relationship, so the parties and/or their attorneys can deal with future differences more easily.

The *Evaluation Criteria Form* for the ABA/LSD Negotiation Competition states that an agreement is not critical to a good score:

While these criteria are helpful in evaluating a particular solution and identifying problems connected with it, they should not be read as requiring that the parties reach agreement. In some situations, e.g., where the opponent's last offer satisfied few of the above criteria, the best outcome might be no agreement at all. Thus, the judging standards focus on planning and the negotiation process itself, allowing a team to achieve a high rating, even if no agreement is reached.

The criteria upon which a negotiation are scored are:

Did the team appear prepared?

Was the team flexible as to be able to adapt its strategy to new information that came to light during the negotiation and to the strategy of the other side?

Did the outcome of the negotiation serve the client interests?

Did the team members demonstrate team work?

Did this team develop a relationship with the other team that detracted from or contribute to its client's best interest?

Did the team promote or violate the ethical requirements of the legal profession?

Based on the team's self-analysis, has this team adequately learned from this negotiation?

Chapter 6

Mediating for Your Client

This chapter deals with skills for the Mediation Advocacy Competition. Generally a mediation competition will involve three rounds with all teams (two students per team) participating in the first two rounds. The four teams with the highest scores advance to the third and final round. This assumes that competition is scaled so the higher the score, the better the performance.

Prior to the competition, all teams receive a set of general facts for all three rounds. Each team also receives confidential facts for the first two rounds of the competition. After the first two rounds are completed, the four teams advancing to the final round will receive confidential facts for that round.

The actual mediation is very dynamic. In a mediation competition, one member of the team is an attorney and the other is the client. The client actively participates in the mediation. Since the client is present, the attorney has the opportunity to caucus with his or her client during the mediation. Each team, however, can only guess the confidential facts of the other side.

The fact that a team has only the general facts and the confidential facts for its side does not mean that little preparation is required. The key to a good performance is preparation.

A. Preparing for the Mediation

A mediation adds a third party to the dispute resolution process. If the disputing parties are unable to resolve their dispute by themselves through negotiation, a neutral third party may be invited to participate in the process. The third party can provide the disputants with a process so their dispute may be resolved. In mediation, the mediator supplies only the process and the parties negotiate through the mediator. The mediator does not resolve the dispute. The ABA's Section of Dispute Resolution Rules direct the mediator to adopt a facilitative rather than an evaluative style of mediator. Therefore, the mediator should assist the parties in working through a process by focusing the discussion on the nature of their problem, their interests, and an array of resolutions for their dispute while refraining from suggesting solutions.

Since mediation is really a negotiation through a third party, the preparation described for a negotiation competition can be followed. Begin by investigating the facts and researching the law followed by applying the law to the facts. Then use the "Worksheet for Dissecting the Content of the Negotiation" to define the problem from your client's perspective and from the other party's perspective, identify your client's interests and other party's interests and identify a range of possible solutions (some favoring all of your client's interests, some favoring the other party's interests, and some favoring both your client's and the other party's interests).

Be prepared to approach the mediation from both an interest based and a position based negotiation posture. The mediator will dictate whether the discussion will follow an interest based or a position based format. Therefore, to be prepared for a position based format, complete the "Position Based (Distributive) Negotiation Worksheet." This will provide you with your client's opening offer, target, and minimum or your client's opening counteroffer, target, and maximum.

B. The Mediation

The mediator will open the joint session of the mediation (both sides are present) with a five minute opening statement that will include an overview of the mediation process, the role of the mediator as a facilitator, the private caucus, the ground rules for the joint session (*e.g.*, one party speaks at a time), and the need for confidentiality.

The mediator may then ask each side to make a brief opening statement. This gives the attorney and client an opportunity to state their perception of the problem and the client's interests. While the client's legal position may be referenced, "the law" should not be the dominant theme since a mediated solution will more likely be non-legal, rather than legal.

The attorney and client must act as a team. Each should participate fully in the mediation. The attorney should act the role of the attorney and the client, the client. Although the attorney will be the more dominant player for the team, the client should have an active role in the mediation. It should also be noted that since the client is the party who is the subject of the dispute, the client will be in a better position to describe the facts and his or her own feelings than the client's attorney.

During the mediation, the mediator will conduct one private caucus with each team. The timing of the caucus will be at the mediator's discretion, although a team may ask to caucus privately with the mediator if that team would like to discuss something with the mediator outside the presence of the other team. If the mediator caucuses with one team, the mediator will caucus with the other. While the mediator is caucusing with one team, the other team will have an opportunity to privately review its strategy.

Since the mediator is acting as a facilitator, the attorneys and their clients will have the opportunity for creative problem-solving. At this point, the possible solution listed on the team's "Worksheet for Dissecting the Content of the Negotiation" becomes important again. Adequate planning will provide a team with multiple suggestions as to outcome and how each possible solution corresponds to the parties' interests. Remember, it is the attorney who advises the client but the client who makes the decision to accept or reject an offer or counteroffer.

If an agreement is reached, it should be reduced to writing. The mediator may decide to draft the document or may ask one of the parties to draft. As in the negotiation, the writing should be as complete as possible. Details omitted from the writing will cause the contract to unravel. Chapter 5 provides guidelines for the writing.

C. The Judges' Grading of the Mediation

The *Judge's Scoring Sheet* for the American Bar Association's Section of Dispute Resolution Mediation Advocacy Competition uses the following criteria to score a mediation:

Did the attorney appear prepared to participate in the mediation and comfortable with the mediation setting?

Did the attorney establish the beginning of a professional and working relationship with the other side and with the mediator?

Did the client appear prepared to participate in the mediation and comfortable with the mediation setting?

Did the attorney appear prepared on the facts and the law and had the attorney analyzed the problem with creativity from both a legal and non-legal prospective?

Did the attorney understand how the other side viewed the problem, including their strengths and weaknesses, and was the attorney able to use this information where appropriate?

Did the attorney and his or her client present the main points of the client's case succinctly and effectively?

Was the attorney effective in articulating the interests of his or her client?

Was the attorney able to work with his or her client in adjusting the client's interests as the mediation evolved?

Did the attorney recognize the interests of the other side?

Was the attorney effective in responding to the mediator and other attorney and was the attorney effective in seeking relevant information?

Was the attorney effective in working with the mediator and the opposing attorney in developing options for mutual gain?

Was the attorney effective in helping his or her client understand the problems and solutions as they arose during the mediation and in making informed choices?

Was the client able to communicate his or her developing and changing needs effectively with his or her attorney during the mediation?

Did the client exhibit confidence in the representation he or she was receiving during the mediation?

Was the client able to introduce new interests and possible solutions into the mediation?

Was the attorney able to adjust to the new interests and possible solutions his or her client introduced into the mediation?

Afterword

In the preceding chapters we have given you step-by-step instructions on how to prepare for a variety of law competitions. Participating in these competitions requires a great deal of time and effort. We congratulate you for making this commitment and wish you great success. We remind you that success is not defined by winning a trophy. *Rather*, success is measured by the analytical and advocacy skills you will acquire through your time and effort. Those skills will serve you well in the practice of law.

Index